YOUNG STUDENTS

Learning Library

VOLUME 1

Aardvark—American History

WEEKLY READER BOOKS
MIDDLETOWN · CONNECTICUT

Young Students Learning Library is a trademark
of Field Publications.

Copyright © 1989, 1988, 1982, 1977 Field Publications;
1974, 1972 by Funk & Wagnalls, Inc. & Field Publications.

ISBN 0-8374-6031-X

EDITORIAL STAFF

ACKNOWLEDGMENTS

STATE OF ALABAMA BUREAU OF PUBLICITY AND INFORMATION page 81(bottom right); 83(top left). JOHN T. ALLEN page 38(top left). ANGLO/CHINESE EDUCATIONAL INSTITUTE page 12(top). AUSTRALIAN NEWS & INFORMATION BUREAU page 53(bottom right). BETTMANN ARCHIVE page 52(top left); 84(bottom left); 85(bottom left); 94(bottom left); 119(top left); 123(bottom left); BRITISH MUSEUM page 115(top right). BUREAU OF INDIAN AFFAIRS page 85(bottom right); 95(bottom right); 100(top left). J. ALLEN CASH page 74(bottom center). CHILDRENS TELEVISION WORKSHOP page 29(top left). COCA COLA page 38(bottom left). DAVE COLLINS page 48(top left). COLONIAL WILLIAMSBURG page 111(bottom right); 113(top right). COLOUR LIBRARY INTERNATIONAL page 113(bottom right). CONNECTICUT HISTORICAL SOCIETY page 124(top). ARMANDO CURCIO EDITORE page 17(bottom right); 20(top); 21(both pics); 23(top right); 24(bottom left); 28(top left); 31(top left); 32(top); 32(bottom left); 34(center left); 36(bottom left); 41(center right); 44(bottom right); 51(top right); 53(top right); 62(top); 65(bottom left); 69(center); 77(bottom center); 75(top right); 88(bottom left); 89(bottom center); 90(bottom); 93(bottom right); 104(top left); 106(bottom); 122(bottom); 125(bottom); 126(top left); 127(top). WALT DISNEY PRODUCTIONS page 28(center); DERBY MUSEUM & ART GALLERY page 93(top left). EDITORIAL PHOTOCOLOR ARCHIVES page 101(top left). FOX-RANK page 28(bottom left). GOODYEAR TIRE & RUBBER COMPANY page 79(bottom left). GREEK TOURIST OFFICE page 26(top left). ROBERT HARDING PICTURE LIBRARY page 77(top left). DAVID HARRIS page 108(top); MICHAEL HOLFORD page 99(top). IMITOR page 108(bottom left). IMPERIAL WAR MUSEUM page 119(top center). INTERNATIONAL HARVESTER COMPANY page 52(center, bottom left, bottom right). JAPAN AIRLINES page 75(top right). LIBRARY OF CONGRESS page 33(top right); 98(bottom left); 105(top left). WILLIAM McQUITTY page 20(bottom right). MANSELL COLLECTION page 111(top right); 118(right center); 118(bottom left). NATIONAL FILM ARCHIVE page 28(top center). NATIONAL MOTOR MUSEUM page 37(bottom right). NATIONAL SCIENCE PHOTOS page 92(P Bowman)(left). NAVAL PHOTO CENTER, WASHINGTON page 59(top right). NASA page 40(top left); 95(top right); 119(bottom right). THE PHILIPS COLLECTION, WASHINGTON page 19(top). PHOTO RESEARCHERS INC. page 102(bottom); (T. McHugh). PHOTOSOURCE page 119(center left); PHOTRI INC. page 109(top right); POPPERFOTO page 120(bottom left); 121(both pics). REDIFFUSION page 65(bottom). ROLLS ROYCE (1971) LTD page 69(top left). SATOUR page 46(top right); 48(bottom). SHELL page 88(top left); SPECTRUM COLOUR LIBRARY page 17(top left); 82(bottom right). TATE GALLERY page 19(bottom right). UNITED STATES AIRFORCE OFFICIAL PHOTOGRAPH page 62(bottom left). UNITED STATES CAPITOL HISTORICAL SOCIETY page 123(top right). UNITED STATES NAVY, OFFICIAL PHOTOGRAPH page 60(top left & bottom left). UNIVERSAL CITY STUDIOS page 27(bottom left). UNIVERSITY OF ILLINOIS AT CHICAGO page 33(center right). JEAN VERTUT page 19(center). JOHN WATNEY page 101(bottom right). ZEFA page 10; 25(top right); 35(top); 39(top left); 42(left center); 46(bottom left); 48(top right); 49(bottom); 54(top left); 56(top left); 59(top right); 64(top right); 72(left); 80(top left); 87(top left); 89(top right); 91(bottom left); 107(top right).

FOREWORD

Growing up in a rapidly changing world is a challenge for every child. YOUNG STUDENTS LEARNING LIBRARY has been written especially for children to enable them to keep pace with the world in which they live.

Children have inquisitive minds. YOUNG STUDENTS LEARNING LIBRARY answers their questions and, at the same time, builds learning skills that last a lifetime. LEARNING LIBRARY is ideal for use at school or at home. Many of the subjects contained in LEARNING LIBRARY support actual lessons children learn in school. Plus, LEARNING LIBRARY is filled with topics that naturally fascinate young people—airplanes, dinosaurs, the human body.

In this 24-volume set, children are introduced to people, places, and events that have shaped their world. The latest information on such topics as AIDS, acid rain, waste disposal, computer technology, fiber optics, and terrorism is written in easy-to-comprehend language. Biographical sketches tell children about famous people who have influenced their lives. Such personalities include: Blaise Pascal, the 17th-century vanguard of computer technology; Susan B. Anthony, champion of women's rights; George Washington Carver, great 19th-century botanist; Mother Teresa, Nobel Peace Prize recipient; Sandra Day O'Connor, first woman Justice of the Supreme Court; and Mikhail Gorbachev, modern-day leader of the Soviet Union.

Children will find YOUNG STUDENTS LEARNING LIBRARY an invaluable reference tool as well as a stimulating and enjoyable reading adventure.

Dr. Terry Borton
Vice President and Editor in Chief

INTRODUCTION

Welcome to the *Young Students Learning Library*. In today's world of rapidly expanding information and discovery, it is crucial for young people to begin as early as possible to understand the dimensions of the world in which they live.

This comprehensive 24 volume library, developed specifically for the needs of elementary-school-age children, makes learning a vitally interactive part of your family life.

More than 3,000 entries are presented in this encyclopedia. Subjects represent basic concepts underlying current elementary school curricula as well as children's outside interests.

Children will find these books accessible, stimulating, activity-oriented, and most important, especially for primary-grade youngsters, non-threatening. Potentially difficult or unfamiliar terms are defined or explained in context. The following special features of this series make this accessibility possible:

READING LEVEL
Parents and educators agree that a child's interest level often exceeds his or her reading level. Therefore, a prime goal of this series is to provide interesting, factual, and readable materials for a wide range of readers. Information is presented on many levels of comprehension to meet the needs of students throughout their elementary and junior high school years. Articles begin with the simplest information and gradually become more detailed as the

text progresses. Charts, up-to-date maps, and more than 5,000 colorful pictures and two-page picture spreads offer the youngest reader a satisfying and stimulating survey of important topics. For the older reader, in-depth coverage offers a more expanded view of a subject. Entries devote considerable attention to biographical and geographical subjects, science and technology, historical and contemporary personalities, countries of the world, U.S. states, and Canadian provinces. While most children will be completely comfortable using this series on their own, younger children will always benefit from the assistance of a parent.

LEARN BY DOING
The activity-oriented Learn By Doing sections are an integral part of this series. Through hands-on involvement, the concepts presented in each book become real and meaningful. The variety of activities suggested in Learn By Doing sections make *Young Students Learning Library* an interactive learning tool, expand a child's understanding of a subject, and stimulate creative thinking. The Learn By Doing activities provide numerous suggestions and step-by-step instructions for completing class projects and have been designed to generate questions and discussions that will produce long-lasting learning. Each Learn By Doing activity is designated by a ■ at the beginning and end of the feature. The entries having Learn By Doing activities are also identi-

fied by asterisks (*) in the index contained in volume 22.

NUGGETS

High points of a topic are presented in capsule form through the Nugget. Printed in bold type in the margin, each Nugget is designated by a wide color-bar for eye-catching appeal. Nuggets contain additional information related to an article and provide children with contrasts, records, trivia, and special examples for selected entries. In addition, the Nugget will make learning more inviting for readers who like to browse. While a reader is flipping pages, the Nugget can grab his or her attention and stimulate a taste for more information.

FULL-COLOR MAPS

New and up-to-date maps of the 50 U.S. states and Canadian provinces have been especially created for this series by Rand McNally. These colorful maps, representing geographical and historical information feature major cities as well as the physical features of states, provinces, and countries. Furthermore, the color scheme for the individual states and provinces shown in each volume is compatible with the same states and provinces shown in the Atlas, a separate volume devoted to maps. The information provided through the maps— like the entries in each volume— has been carefully selected to correlate with school curricula, making *Young Students Learning Library* a most practical learning tool.

HOW TO READ THE MAPS

Each map features:
- A scale bar and a north arrow,
- Major rivers, lakes and mountain ranges,
- A prominent star indicating each state capital,
- Major national parks,
- Boundaries of surrounding states, including state names and very major cities.

In addition to the foregoing, *Young Students Learning Library* includes the following important elements:
- More than 3,000 articles arranged in alphabetical order, letter by letter, except when a comma appears in the title. For example, **CAT, WILD,** appears before **CATACOMBS,** but **HORSEPOWER** appears before **HORSE RACING.**
- An interlacing chain of cross-references that guide the young student to related information. At the ends of articles, they appear as ALSO READ: followed by one or more article titles. In alphabetical order, where a subject might be expected to appear but instead has been incorporated into another article, a slightly different form of cross-reference has been used; for example, **ACCIDENT PREVENTION** see SAFETY, or **ADENOIDS** see BREATHING.
- Traditional measurements along with the metric equivalents are located throughout each volume.
- An index, located in Volume

22, provides more than 20,000 entries. Complete directions for the best use of the index appear at its start in the last volume.

- Tables of information and fact boxes with each U.S. President, U.S. state, Canadian province, and nations that highlight important data about each.
- Glossaries of terms commonly used in relation to the subject of an article. For examples, see **BOXING, CATTLE** or **MUSIC.**
- A dictionary that contains 34,000 entries and 1,400 illustrations.
- An atlas, written exclusively by Rand McNally for *Young Students Learning Library* that contains up-to-date maps and information.

Designed for use at home or in school, *Young Students Learning Library* provides children with a basic information and activities source for their pleasure and enlightenment. Regular use of this library will develop an exciting and rewarding foundation for every child's future.

CONTENTS

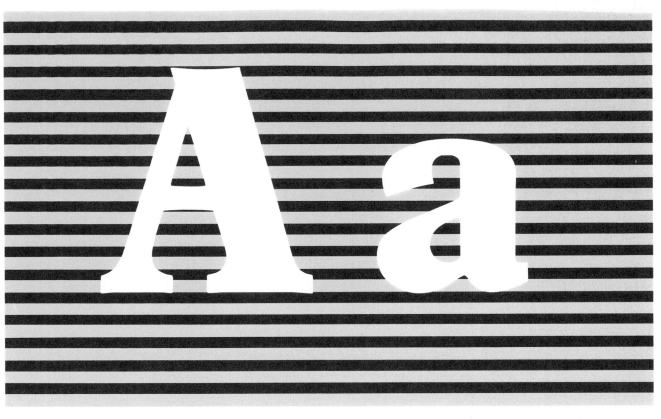

AARDVARK The aardvark is a strange animal of Africa. It is so unusual that scientists place it in an order of mammals by itself—order Tubulidentata, which means "tube-toothed." Its teeth have no roots or strong enamel. But the aardvark does not really need strong teeth because it eats only termites and ants.

The aardvark grows up to 6 feet (1.8 m) long, including its thick tail. Very few bristly hairs can be seen on its pinkish-gray skin, although some aardvarks have long, full coats of hair. The aardvark's narrow head is topped by large rabbit-like ears. Its ears can pick up the faint sounds made by termites in their nests. The aardvark uses its strong front claws to tear open the hard mud-mound nests of termites. The insects attack the aardvark, but not even their sharp pincers can go through its tough skin. The aardvark catches the termites with its long, sticky tongue. The aardvark

also uses its claws to dig a home underground. It digs a deep burrow, where it hides from enemies and sleeps during the day, coming out to hunt for food at night. If attacked, it lies on its back and uses its claws to defend itself.

Dutch settlers in South Africa gave it the name aardvark, which means "earth pig." It is also called "ant bear." Aardvarks live throughout Africa south of the Sahara.

ALSO READ: ANTEATER, MAMMAL.

If caught away from its burrow, the aardvark digs a hole for itself at astonishing speed, earth and stones flying out from its powerful front feet to a height of some 14 feet (4 m).

▼ *The aardvark is a mammal that lives in the dry parts of Africa. It uses its long tongue to catch termites.*

◀ *African camel riders, from the Sahel region.* (See AFRICA.)

ABACUS An abacus is a device that helps a person count and do arithmetic problems. As you can see in the diagram, an abacus uses beads to keep track of the numbers. The beads slide along rods. Each rod has seven beads—five on the left and two on the right of the center strip. Before starting to solve a problem, the beads should be pushed away from the center strip, because that is where the numbers are counted.

The more rows of beads on an abacus, the larger the numbers you can count. Each row stands for a different *power of ten*. Powers of ten are 1, 10, 100, 1,000, and so on, adding as many zeros as you like.

The five beads on the left in every row each stand for *one* of the unit of that row. The two beads on the right are each *five* of the unit. Numbers are formed by bringing the beads from their starting position to the center strip. To count a number on an

▲ *Chinese schoolchildren are still taught to use the abacus.*

abacus, you push enough beads into the center to equal your number. To subtract a number, you push the right number of beads away from the center.

■ **LEARN BY DOING**

You can make an abacus. You will need a picture frame, string, beads, and thumbtacks. Many abacuses have 13 rows of beads. But you can make a smaller one, with only five rows, and still count up to 166,665. To make a five-row abacus, first cut five pieces of string the same length—long enough to cross the picture frame plus 3 inches (7.6 cm) for tying knots. Tie a knot one-fourth of the way down each piece of string. Make the knots fat, so no beads can pass them. The knots will be the center strip in your abacus. Now carefully put five evenly spaced thumbtacks on each side of the picture frame. Slide five beads onto one string at the end that is farther from the knot. Put two beads onto the short end. Tie the ends of the string to the first thumbtack on either side of the frame, with the group of five

▼ *These pictures show some western abacuses with three rows of beads. But some abacuses have more rows. You can tell that no adding is being done on the top abacus. No beads are touching the center strip. A real abacus does not have the numbers written on the beads as this one does. Each abacus in the six lower drawings shows a different number—(a) 3; (b) 7; (d) 73; and (e) 98. Can you work out what numbers abacus (c) and abacus (f) show?*

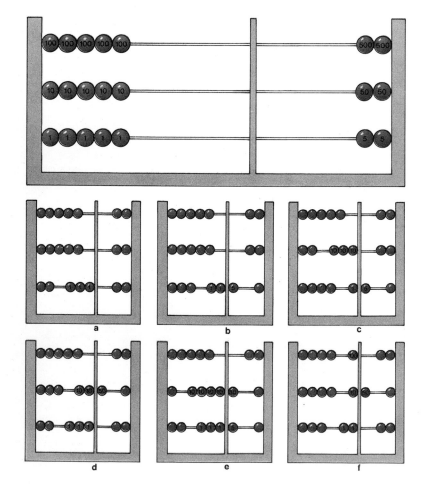

beads at the left. Then load the other four strings with beads and tie them to the other four pairs of tacks.

Hold your abacus flat, with the groups of five beads toward your left, and you are ready to try a simple problem. First, count 3 on your abacus. Push three beads on the bottom row to the right until they touch the center strip (the knot). Now add 5. Do this by pushing one right-hand bead on the bottom row to the left until it touches the center strip, too. You have just completed an addition problem. What is the total? Now try subtracting 6 from the total. What answer do you get? (Remember, to subtract, you push the right number of beads *away* from the center strip.) Next, add 210 to the number on your abacus. You can read this number in three parts—two hundreds (200), one ten (10), and no ones (0). If you work carefully, the total that your abacus shows will be 212. You will find you can solve difficult problems with the help of your abacus. ■

Bead abacuses like this were used in ancient China. The ancient Egyptians, Greeks, and Romans used a kind of abacus that had pebbles or other movable counters. Today, the abacus has largely been replaced by the electronic calculator, but it is still used for calculating in the Middle East and in parts of Asia. It is also especially useful for teaching blind children to calculate.

ALSO READ: ARITHMETIC, CALCULATOR, COMPUTER.

ABBREVIATION To abbreviate means to make shorter. Words and phrases are often shortened to save time and space in speaking and writing. Abbreviations, acronyms, and contractions are some ways of shortening language.

Abbreviations are letters that stand for common, well-known words and

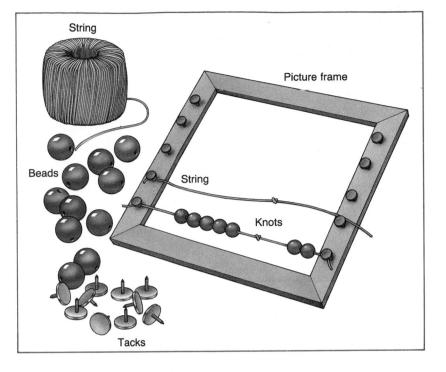

String

Picture frame

Beads

String

Knots

Tacks

phrases. Sometimes, the letters have periods after them to show that other letters have been left out. There are no basic rules for forming abbreviations. Perhaps somebody just decided to shorten a word or phrase in a certain way. It soon became accepted and understood. Sometimes just the beginning of the word is used, such as *doz.* for "dozen" or *max.* for "maximum." Other abbreviations use the first and last letters, such as *Rd.* for "Road" or *Dr.* for "Doctor." And still others use just the first letter: for example, *m* stands for "meter."

Some abbreviations do not look like the words they stand for. Such abbreviations usually come from ancient Latin or Greek words or from modern foreign languages. *A.M.* means "before noon." It is an abbreviation of the Latin *ante meridiem.* The shortened form for *pound* is *lb.,* from the Latin word *libra,* which was a unit of weight. *R.S.V.P.* (on an invitation) means "Please reply." It stands for the French words, *Répondez, s'il vous plaît.*

Abbreviated words can be confusing. Several words may share the same abbreviation. The letters *St.* can mean either "Street" or "Saint." And

Many of the words we use today are abbreviations. We seldom stop to think that bus is short for omnibus, flu for influenza, zoo for zoological gardens, and cello for violoncello.

SOME COMMON ABBREVIATIONS

A.A. Alcoholics Anonymous
AAA American Automobile Association
abbr. abbreviation
ABC American Broadcasting Company
A.D. *anno Domini,* "in the year of our Lord"
adj. adjective
adv. adverb; advertisement
AFL-CIO American Federation of Labor and Congress of Industrial Organizations
Ala., AL Alabama
Alas., AK Alaska
A.M., a.m. *ante meridiem,* "before noon"
anon. anonymous, "author unknown"
AP Associated Press
Apr. April
Ariz., AZ Arizona
Ark., AR Arkansas
assn. association
asst. assistant
atty. Attorney
Aug. August
Ave. Avenue
A.W.O.L. absent without leave
b. born
BBC British Broadcasting Corporation
B.C. before Christ; British Columbia
bldg. building
Blvd. Boulevard
bros. brothers
c. *circa,* about
C Celsius; centigrade
Calif., CA California
CBC Canadian Broadcasting Corporation
CBS Columbia Broadcasting System
cc cubic centimeter
cm centimeter
Co. Company; County
c/o in care of
C.O.D. cash on delivery
Colo., CO Colorado
conj. conjunction
Conn., CT Connecticut
cont. continued
Corp. Corporation
CPA Certified Public Accountant
CST Central Standard Time
d. died
D.A. District Attorney
DAR Daughters of the American Revolution
D.A.V. Disabled American Veterans
D.C., DC District of Columbia
D.D.S. Doctor of Dental Surgery
Dec. December
Del., DE Delaware
Dem. Democrat
Dr. Doctor; Drive
DST Daylight Saving Time
E. east
e.g. *exempli gratia,* "for example"
Eng. English; England
EST Eastern Standard Time
etc. *et cetera,* "and so forth"
F Fahrenheit
FDIC Federal Deposit Insurance Corporation
Feb. February
Fla., FL Florida
Fr. Father; French; France

Fri. Friday
ft. foot; feet
Ft. Fort
g gram
Ga., GA Georgia
Gov. Governor
H.I., HI Hawaii
Hon. Honorable
HRH His (Her) Royal Highness
I. Island
Ia., IA Iowa
ibid. *ibidem,* in the same place
Id., ID Idaho
i.e. *id est,* "that is," "in other words"
ill., illus. illustration
Ill., IL Illinois
in. inch; inches
Inc. Incorporated
Ind., IN Indiana
IOU I owe you
IQ intelligence quotient
Jan. January
Jr. Junior
Kans., KS Kansas
kg kilogram
km kilometer
Ky., KY Kentucky
l liter
La., LA Louisiana
m meter
Mar. March
Mass., MA Massachusetts
M.D. Doctor of Medicine
Md., MD Maryland
Me., ME Maine
Mich., MI Michigan
Minn., MN Minnesota
Miss., MS Mississippi
ml milliliter
Mlle. Mademoiselle
mm millimeter
Mo., MO Missouri
Mon. Monday
Mont., MT Montana
mpg miles per gallon
mph miles per hour
Mr. Mister
Mrs. Mistress (used for a married woman)
Ms. written form of address for any woman
MST Mountain Standard Time
Mt. Mount; Mountain
n. noun
N. north
NASA National Aeronautics and Space Administration
NATO North Atlantic Treaty Organization
NBC National Broadcasting Company
N.C., NC North Carolina
N.Dak., ND North Dakota
Nebr., NB Nebraska
Nev., NV Nevada
N.H., NH New Hampshire
N.J., NJ New Jersey
N.Mex., NM New Mexico
no. number
Nov. November
N.Y., NY New York
O., OH Ohio
Oct. October
Okla., OK Oklahoma

Ore., OR Oregon
p. page
Pa., Penn., PA Pennsylvania
pat. patent
PBS Public Broadcasting Service
P.D. police department; postal district
Pfc. Private first class
pl. plural
Pl. Place
P.M., p.m. *post meridiem,* "after noon"; *post mortem,* "after death"
P.O. post office
POW prisoner of war
pp. pages
prep. preposition
pron. pronoun
P.S. *post scriptum,* "postscript"; Public School
PST Pacific Standard Time
R. River
Rd. Road
Rep. Republican
Rev. Reverend; Revelations
R.I., RI Rhode Island
rpm revolutions per minute
R.R. railroad
R.S.V.P. *Répondez, s'il vous plaît,* "please reply"
S. south
SAC Strategic Air Command
Sat. Saturday
S.C., SC South Carolina
S.Dak., SD South Dakota
Sept. September
sing. singular
S.P.C.A. Society for the Prevention of Cruelty to Animals
sq. square
Sr. Senior
S.S. steamship
St. Saint; Street
Sun. Sunday
Tenn., TN Tennessee
Terr. Terrace; Territory
Tex., TX Texas
Thur., Thurs. Thursday
TNT trinitrotoluene
Tues. Tuesday
U., UT Utah
UHF ultra-high frequency
UN United Nations
UNICEF United Nations Children's Fund
UPI United Press International
U.S. United States
U.S.A. United States of America
U.S.S.R. Union of Soviet Socialist Republics
v. verb
Va., VA Virginia
VHF very high frequency
VI Virgin Islands
VIP very important person
Vt., VT Vermont
W. west
Wash., WA Washington
Wed. Wednesday
Wis., WI Wisconsin
W.Va., WV West Virginia
Wyo., WY Wyoming
YMCA Young Men's Christian Association
YWCA Young Women's Christian Association

Fr. may mean "Father," "France," or "French." It is up to the reader to decide what an abbreviation means by looking at the rest of the sentence.

An *acronym* is an abbreviation that is actually a word, because it can be easily pronounced. *NATO,* for example, is an acronym for *North Atlantic Treaty Organization. NASA* stands for *National Aeronautics and Space Administration.*

A *contraction* is a shortened phrase that, when written, has an apostrophe to show that letters are missing. Contractions, such as "isn't" and "won't," are used more often in speaking than in writing.

■ LEARN BY DOING

You probably know more abbreviations than you think you do. Find out. Print one letter of the alphabet on each of 26 small pieces of paper. Mix them up in a bag and draw five pieces of paper. How many different abbreviations can you make from the five letters you drew? Have a contest with a friend and see who can make the most abbreviations. ■

In the list of common abbreviations with this article, the regular shortened form of a state's name is followed by the official two-letter U.S. Postal Service abbreviation. For example, Minn. and MN are shown for Minnesota.

ALSO READ: WRITTEN LANGUAGE.

ABOLITION Slaves were first brought to North America during the 1600's. Even then, there were people who thought that slavery was wrong. These people were part of the *antislavery* movement, which grew both in Europe and in the United States. By the 1800's, a growing number of people in the United States were outraged about slavery. These people refused to obey laws that helped slave owners. They hid runaway slaves.

They gave speeches and wrote books and newspaper articles against slavery. They decided that slavery had to be *abolished* (ended) as quickly as possible. These people were called *abolitionists.*

One of the most famous abolitionists was William Lloyd Garrison. From 1831 to the end of the Civil War in 1865, he published an anti-slavery newspaper called *The Liberator.* Another important abolitionist was Frederick Douglass, a black journalist. His newspaper, *The North Star,* urged blacks and whites to help slaves escape from the South. Charles Lenox Remond, a black abolitionist speaker, traveled through the country, speaking against slavery wherever people would listen.

Harriet Beecher Stowe wrote *Uncle Tom's Cabin* in 1852. This novel told a dramatic tale of how slaves were forced to live. It told about beatings and about how slave families were separated when the mother or father was sold to another slave owner. The book made many people examine their own attitudes toward slavery.

Some people did not like the abolitionists. People threw stones and rotten eggs at William Lloyd Garrison when he made speeches against slavery. An angry mob in Boston once dragged him through the streets. Another abolitionist editor, Elijah P. Lovejoy, was murdered by a mob.

Some people thought that speaking and writing against slavery was not enough. John Brown tried to convince the slaves to start a revolution. In 1859, he and some followers captured the U.S. arsenal, a place where guns and ammunition were kept, at Harpers Ferry, Virginia (now in West Virginia). He hoped the raid would be a signal to all slaves to fight for their freedom. But many of his followers were killed by soldiers. Brown was captured and hanged for treason.

People who were afraid of abolitionists lived all over the U.S. They thought abolitionists caused trouble

▲ *Charles Lenox Remond, a respected black speaker for abolition.*

In the days before the Civil War, about 50,000 slaves escaped from the South to the North. Most of them traveled by the Underground Railroad—a system for helping slaves to travel from one safe hiding place to another. The Underground Railroad was centered in Pennsylvania and Ohio.

15

▲ *The abominable snowman is also known as the yeti. The British mountaineer Eric Shipton photographed 'yeti' tracks which he found in snow near Mount Everest in 1951.*

Some aborigines believed that they could kill an enemy by pointing a sharpened bone at him, while singing a death chant. They believed that an invisible bone splinter flew into the victim's body without leaving a mark on the skin. Often the victim died out of sheer terror unless a witch doctor could be found to magic away the invisible piece of bone.

and did not try to find a workable solution to the problem. Some Southerners tried to silence the abolitionists, even in Congress. But those who spoke out boldly against slavery finally won their battle. On January 1, 1863, President Abraham Lincoln made his Emancipation Proclamation, freeing the slaves in the Confederate States. The Thirteenth Amendment was added to the U.S. Constitution in 1865, and slaves were freed in all of the United States.

ALSO READ: BROWN, JOHN; CIVIL WAR; DOUGLASS, FREDERICK; EMANCIPATION PROCLAMATION; SLAVERY; STOWE, HARRIET BEECHER; UNDERGROUND RAILROAD.

ABOMINABLE SNOWMAN

The abominable snowman is a creature some people believe lives high in the Himalaya Mountains of Asia. The people of Tibet call the snowman the *yeti*. Local stories tell of a large, hairy beast with arms that hang to its knees. It walks upright, on its back legs, and has a humanlike face. The yeti is supposed to leave the snowy regions from time to time, and come down to attack villagers. However, no one has yet proved that the yeti exists.

Many people have seen large, strange footprints in the snow of the Himalayas. Some people believe these are the yeti's prints. Others think they are footprints of a running bear, whose hind feet may land partly on the prints made by its front feet. These two sets of prints may, together, look like a large human print. Other large prints are probably formed when snow melts around a group of several small animal footprints. Since the 1890's, several explorers of the Himalayas have seen huge footprints of a large, unknown creature. The Tibetans have pieces of hair and dried scalp, which they claim are from the yeti. But scientists know these pieces are from bears, yaks, antelopes, and other animals.

Sir Edmund Hillary, an explorer, led an expedition to the Himalayas in 1960, to search for the creature. No abominable snowman was found. It does not seem likely that a large ape, or similar animal, could live in such high and snowy regions, where food is scarce. Yet, there are stories of similar strange creatures in other parts of the world. Some people claim to have seen a hairy, humanlike animal in the forests of the northwestern United States. They call it *Bigfoot*, for its large "footprints." But, as with the abominable snowman, no one has proved that this creature really exists. People enjoy stories about legendary animals, such as the abominable snowman and Bigfoot, even though such stories rarely turn out to be true.

ALSO READ: ANIMALS OF MYTH AND LEGEND; HILLARY, SIR EDMUND; HIMALAYA MOUNTAINS.

ABORIGINE   The first people to live in any region are called *aborigines*. The term comes from the Latin words, *ab origine*, which mean "from the beginning."

The name *aborigine* or *aboriginal* is most often given to the earliest known people of Australia. These people were living in Australia when Europeans began to explore that continent in the 1700's. Scientists call these aborigines *Australoids*. They moved to Australia from Southeast Asia 12,000 years ago.

Between 150,000 and 300,000 aborigines lived in Australia when Europeans settled there in 1788. Now there are only 40,000 pure aborigines. Many were killed by diseases brought by white settlers, who sometimes took away their land. Most aborigines now live among nonaborigines, often working on cattle and sheep ranches and in factories and offices. Others have kept their old tribal ways of life,

▲ *An Australian aborigine* boomerang *and shield.*

living on reservations in the Northern Territory, Queensland, and Western Australia. The aborigines have sought the return of some of their tribal lands. Their hunting weapons are the *boomerang*, the *waddy* (a war club), and the *woomera* (a throwing stick with a three-pronged spear in front). They are expert at tracking and finding food in the wilderness.

The aborigines have always lived close to nature. They know the secret ways of animals and plants, and their colorful rock paintings are full of beauty and magical meaning. Aborigines believe that ancestral spirits live in certain places. One of these tribal "spirit homes" is Ayers Rock, now protected as an aborigine monument.

ALSO READ: AUSTRALIA.

ABRASIVES If you want to make a rough piece of wood smooth, what do you do? You rub it with sandpaper. The tiny, hard bits of sand in the sandpaper are *abrasives*. They wear away the roughness of the wood, which is softer.

Abrasives are materials used to smooth, polish, grind, or cut other substances. Most abrasives are minerals. The hardest of all minerals is diamond, so this makes the best abrasive. But diamond is very expensive. Sandpaper is made of bits of quartz, which costs a lot less.

Some abrasives are formed naturally in the earth. Quartz, diamond, sand, and pumice are all natural abrasives. Carborundum is a manufactured abrasive. It is made from a mixture of clay and powdered coke heated in a furnace. Carborundum is so hard that it can easily scratch glass, and for this reason it is used to polish gemstones.

Big blocks of abrasive material have been used since ancient times to make grindstones, to sharpen knives, and to mill grain. Another use for abrasives is to clean buildings. A jet of sand and metal particles is blown by compressed air to scrub away the soot and grime on the walls. This is known as "sandblasting." The tips, or cutting edges, of drills are covered with tiny pieces of tough abrasive. An oil well drill can cut through rock be-

▲ *An Australian aborigine. At one time all the people of Australia were aborigines. But now there are only about 40,000 full-blooded aborigines in the country.*

Toothpaste usually contains a mild abrasive—generally fine powdered chalk. The oldest abrasive is sand. It was used to polish stone weapons as early as 25,000 B.C. Diamond, the hardest known substance, was used as an abrasive in India by 700 B.C.

Dark objects absorb more light and heat than light objects do. This explains why people in hot countries usually wear white clothes. The heat tends to bounce off them. It also explains why houses in hot countries tend to be painted in light colors.

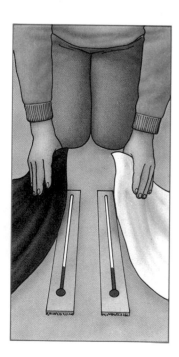

cause of the tiny abrasive diamonds in its cutting edge.

■ LEARN BY DOING

If you build models, then you have probably used sandpaper. Have you noticed how sandpaper comes in different grades? Get a piece of board. Sand sections of it with three different grades of sandpaper. Compare each section carefully. What did you find? ■

ABSORPTION

Liquid spilled on a table top can be soaked up by a sponge, a napkin, or a paper towel. This soaking up is absorption. Many things can be soaked up, or absorbed, by other substances or objects. Gas, liquid, light, heat, and even sound can be absorbed.

Let a glass of *cold* water stand in sunlight. You will see small air bubbles form on the sides of the glass. The bubbles rise through the water to the surface. These bubbles are air that was absorbed in the water. The air was forced out as the water warmed up because warm water cannot hold so much air as cold water can.

Absorption is an important process for living things. Fish breathe the air that is absorbed in water. In humans and other animals, digested food is absorbed by the blood through the vessels of the small intestine and then carried to all parts of the body where it is used for energy. Plants absorb water from the soil. The water keeps them alive and healthy. What happens if you put a partly wilted flower in a glass of water?

■ LEARN BY DOING

Light and heat can be absorbed too. Dark objects are better heat and light absorbers than light-colored ones. You can prove this with a simple experiment. On a cold, sunny day, put two thermometers on the ground. Be sure they show the same temperature. Put a black cloth over

one and a white one over the other. Which thermometer shows the highest temperature after half an hour? ■

ALSO READ: COLOR, DIGESTION, GAS, HEAT AND COLD, LIGHT, LIQUID, PLANT, SOUND.

ABSTRACT ART

You probably know that "subtract" means "take away." *Abstract* means "to take what is important away from what is not." Abstract art shows what is important in a scene and leaves out unimportant details.

Look at the picture of the horse on the next page. It was painted on the wall of a cave near Lascaux, France, thousands of years ago. It is a simple painting. The cave artist left out details. He arranged the horse to fit the picture, not as it really looked wandering around outside his cave. The picture is *not* "realistic," just like life. It is *abstract art*.

In the 1880's in France, some artists began to make painting less realistic. Why? For one thing, the camera had been invented. A photograph could be made to get an exact likeness of something or someone. So the French painters began new ways of painting. "Looking like something" became less important. Two French painters, Paul Cézanne and Georges Seurat, found that people could see the shapes of nature more easily if the shapes were painted simply, without all the details used in realistic art.

Some years later another artist, Pablo Picasso, began to paint abstractly, too. Only he went much further. He would change nature to what he thought a picture should be. He tried in his paintings to show more than the appearance of an object, to seek new meaning. Sculpture too could be abstract. Artists ignored the exact form of a real-life object. The feel and texture and shape of a sculpture were more important to abstract artists than showing exact form.

▲ Arrival of the Circus *by Paul Klee.*

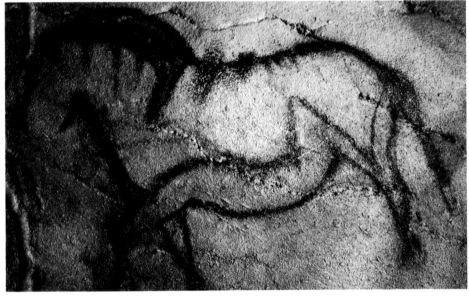

◀ *A Stone Age painting of a horse in a cave at Lascaux, France.*

▲ *Piet Mondrian's* Composition in Red, Yellow and Blue.

■ LEARN BY DOING

Look at Paul Klee's painting of a circus arriving in town. See the circus parade with a dog leading it? The painter uses no perspective in this picture, so things that might be farther away don't look smaller. Instead, the picture is in layers. Nearly everyone in the painting is wearing a funny hat. Why? Many things are happening at the same time, as in a real circus. Look for details, such as the boy holding a balloon over his head. Banners often mean fun and excitement. How many do you see here? See how Klee has "framed" his picture with dark paint in a smudgy way. Is the picture a dream of long ago?

How would your community look if a circus were arriving? Make a picture of it on a big piece of paper. Is your painting an abstract one, rather than a realistic one?

Do you see the horse in the Jackson

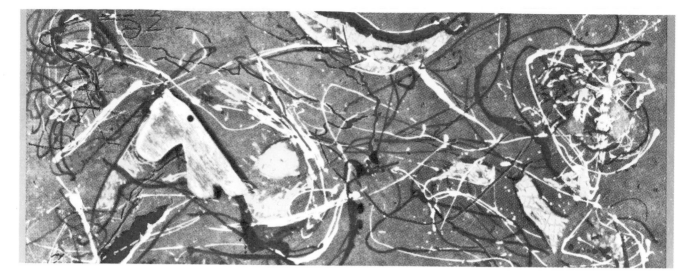

▲ *Jackson Pollock's* The Wooden Horse.

▼ *A drawing of Marcel Duchamp's* Bicycle Wheel, *1913. Duchamp fixed the wheel to a kitchen stool. The original no longer exists.*

Pollock painting, *The Wooden Horse?* What does the rest of the picture look like to you? Could those tangled lines be paths the horse followed? The yellow splotches could be places where the horse rested. Do the red lines show a really fast ride? Think what fun it would be to take off along those trails. See if you can paint a picture story of an exciting horseback ride.

Look at Marcel Duchamp's sculpture—a bicycle wheel mounted on a kitchen stool. He called these sculptures "ready-mades." Can you put together your own ready-made? ■

Of course, you may see Pollock's painting in a very different way. That is the fun of abstract art. You can see it in a new way every time you look at it. Abstract art can be more exciting than a realistic painting or sculpture which looks exactly like the real scene or object every time you see it. A photograph shows you a scene. An abstract painting can show you more.

ALSO READ: CÉZANNE, PAUL; MODERN ART; PICASSO, PABLO; REALISM; SCULPTURE.

ABU SIMBEL Abu Simbel is the site of two ancient temples on the Nile River in Egypt. The temples were carved into a sandstone cliff about 1250 B.C. by order of Ramses II, an Egyptian pharaoh (king).

The Great Temple reached over 180 feet (55 m) into the side of the cliff. The entrance was guarded by four statues of Ramses II. Each statue was 67 feet (20 m) high. Ramses II wished to honor the sun god. The pharaoh had the temple built so that the sun's early-morning rays shone through the halls and touched the carved figure of the sun god deep inside. The smaller temple had six figures, each 33 feet (10.2 m) high, at

▶ *The giant statues of the Temple of Abu Simbel used to stand beside the Nile River. When the Aswan Dam was built they were moved to higher ground.*

its entrance. Four were of Ramses II and two were of his queen, Nefertari.

Egypt planned a great dam on the Nile River in the 1960's. But the plan called for the valley of the temples to be flooded. Egypt asked the United Nations to help save the temples before the dam was built. More than 50 nations helped fund the project. The temples were cut into huge blocks. The blocks were moved to high, safe ground and put together again. Egypt finished the Aswan High Dam in 1968, and a lake now covers the old site.

ALSO READ: EGYPT, ANCIENT; NILE RIVER.

ACADEMY AWARD The Academy of Motion Picture Arts and Sciences was founded in 1927 by Louis B. Mayer and other leaders of the Hollywood film world. The Academy is made up of several thousand people in every area of movie making. Its main purpose is to help improve the art and science of film making. The Academy also honors outstanding film achievements with its Academy Awards. The Academy members vote on who should win.

Once each year in Hollywood, California, small gold statues are awarded for the best performances by actors and actresses in leading and supporting roles and for best direction, music, costume design, photography, writing, sound recording, and other areas of production. An award is also given for the best movie of the year. Each award is a statue of a man, nicknamed "Oscar."

The first movie to win an Oscar was *Wings* in 1928. The first film to capture all five major awards (Best Picture, Best Actor, Best Actress, Best Director, and Best Screenplay) was *It Happened One Night*, starring Claudette Colbert and Clark Gable, which did so in 1934. Today, the Oscar ceremony is a much publicized

event. Winning can mean box office success as well as artistic acclaim.

ALSO READ: ACTORS AND ACTING, MOTION PICTURES.

ACANTHUS   see GREEK ART.

ACCELERATION   see MOTION.

ACCELERATOR   see PARTICLE ACCELERATOR.

ACCIDENT PREVENTION   see SAFETY.

ACCORDION   An accordion is a musical instrument that works like a reed-organ. The accordion hangs by straps from the player's shoulders.

The first accordion-like instrument was made by Friedrich Buschmann in Germany in 1822. An Austrian, Cyril Demian, soon made some improvements, and gave the instrument its name. About the same time, Charles Wheatstone of England invented the concertina, which is like the accordion.

The accordion is mainly a bellows. The player stretches the bellows to let in air. He then closes, or squeezes, the bellows, and the air is forced out through metal parts called *tongues* or *reeds*. These tongues are of different sizes, so they produce different musical notes. The piano accordion has, attached to the bellows on the right side, a keyboard like that of a piano. The accordionist plays the melody on the keyboard. On the left are buttons which he presses to produce bass notes and chords.

Pioneers traveling West in the 1800's enjoyed accordion music.

ALSO READ: MUSICAL INSTRUMENTS, ORGAN.

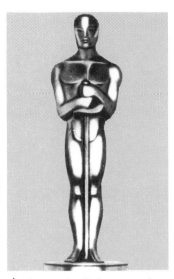

▲ Oscar, the little statue given as an Academy Award, stands 13½ inches (34 cm) high.

In 1931, the Academy Award statue was accidentally nicknamed "Oscar" by Academy librarian Margaret Herrick. When she first saw the statue, she said, "Why, it looks like my Uncle Oscar!" A newspaperman heard her remark and printed it in his newspaper.

▲ An accordion is like an organ. The player squeezes the bellows in and out while playing a melody on the keys.

ACCOUNTING AND BOOK-KEEPING Business people must keep records of the money they take in and the money they spend. The work of keeping such records is called *bookkeeping*. The work of deciding how the records should be set up is called *accounting*. An *accountant* also finds out, from the records, whether or not a business is doing well.

Suppose a man owns a small clothing store. He keeps records that show that he spent money for newspaper advertising, and for suits, coats, shirts, shoes, and neckties to sell to his customers. He had to pay a young man to help him in the store. He also paid rent and had other expenses.

At the end of the year, he must take an *inventory*. That is, he counts how many pieces of clothing he has on hand. Then he must find out exactly how many he sold, how much money he took in, and how much money he spent in running the business. If he took in more than he spent, he made a *profit* for the year. If he spent more than he took in, he suffered a *loss*.

The owner of a small clothing store can keep accounting records without much trouble. But a giant oil company or a big bank has many difficult accounting problems. The company must know how much money is to be paid by its *debtors* (people who owe the company money) and how much it owes other companies (*creditors*) for supplies. It must know how much the company's buildings and machines are worth, and how much the com-

pany has lost in *depreciation*, or wear and tear, of its equipment. All of this information must be kept in the company's accounts. Big companies employ many accountants.

After a company's accountants finish their yearly count, their work must be *audited*. Experts from outside the company double-check the records to be sure the accounts are correct. These experts are called *auditors*.

■ **LEARN BY DOING**
You can practice bookkeeping by keeping records of your own money. Suppose your weekly allowance is 3 dollars and 75 cents. Your grandmother gives you 5 dollars as a gift. A piece of candy costs you 50 cents, and a balsa-wood glider costs 2 dollars and 95 cents. You want to go to the movies on Saturday, and you also want to save some money.

Make a chart with three columns on a lined sheet of paper. Mark the first column "Received," the second column "Spent," and the third column "Balance" (meaning the money you have left). What numbers go in what columns? How much money will you be able to save if the movies cost you two dollars? ■

This is a simple bookkeeping system. It is a record of money received, or *income*, and money paid out, or *expenses*. Your parents may keep records like this of home expenses.

Today, many bookkeeping and accounting records are made by computers. But people still have to provide the information the machines need to do the jobs.

ALSO READ: CALCULATOR, ECONOMICS, MONEY.

ACHILLES see TROJAN WAR.

ACID RAIN Rain is always slightly acid. This is because the Earth's at-

Acid rain is not new. People have known about it for quite a long time. In 1858 the British chemist Robert Angus Smith presented a paper to the Chemical Society. In it he spoke of how "the stones and bricks of buildings crumble more readily in large towns where much more coal is burned, than elsewhere." He said that this was caused by "the slow but constant action of the acid rain." This was the first time that the term "acid rain" was used.

mosphere naturally contains substances such as carbon dioxide and sulfur dioxide, which dissolve in moisture to form weak acids. When we burn fossil fuels, such as coal and oil, either in factories or automobile engines, extra amounts of chemicals are added to the atmosphere. Some of these chemicals can form acids. When clouds gather, the rain that falls has a higher than normal acid content. It is called *acid rain.*

Dirt put into the air in one part of the world can affect other places, thousands of miles away. If a factory in one country gives off too much dirt, acid rain may fall somewhere else. Scientists are not in agreement on what harm is done by acid rain. Trees and soil and fish may suffer, and so may buildings, since acid eats into stone.

Acid rain, like other kinds of air pollution, can be checked in several ways. Low-sulfur fuels can be burnt. Automobiles that burn lead-free gasoline are cleaner than automobiles that do not. The smokestacks of power stations can be fitted with special equipment to scrub clean smoke and gases before they are released into the air.

ALSO READ: ACIDS AND BASES, AIR POLLUTION, RAIN AND SNOW, WATER CYCLE.

ACIDS AND BASES Have you ever tasted an unripe apple? It has a sour taste. Lemons are sour. Vinegar is sour, too. What makes things taste sour? The answer is, they all have acid in them. There are many kinds of acid. Some are very strong and can eat their way through almost anything. *Sulfuric acid,* for example, can *corrode* (eat into) most metals and it will quickly burn into flesh or other living matter. *Nitric acid* and *hydrochloric acid* are two other strong acids. These strong acids are among the most important of all chemicals used in industry. Automobile batteries are full of dilute sulfuric acid—acid that has been mixed with water to make it less strong.

But not all acids are strong and dangerous. Yogurt, for example, contains acid, and so does aspirin. Our own bodies make many acids to digest food and build new tissue.

Bases are substances that are the opposite of acids. Some bases are strong and corrosive too. Substances such as caustic soda and lime are strong bases. Caustic soda is often used for cleaning the insides of stoves because it has a powerful action in removing grease. Weak bases include baking soda and magnesium hydroxide, the white powder or liquid we take to cure an upset acid stomach.

Another name for a base is an *alkali,* although strictly speaking an alkali is a base that can dissolve in water.

When an acid and a base are mixed together in the right quantities they *neutralize* each other—cancel each other out in some ways. If we mix hydrochloric acid and caustic soda, for example, both very strong and dangerous substances, the result is harmless common salt and water. Acids and bases always react together to give some kind of salt and water.

Some substances change color when they are put into an acid or base. One of these is a dye called *litmus.* Litmus paper turns red if dipped into anything acid. It turns blue if dipped into a base. So litmus makes a good test for acids and bases.

▲ *Two hydrangea flowers. Chemicals in the soil act on a substance in the flowers called* pigment *to produce the different colors. Alkaline (basic) soil produces pink hydrangeas. Acid in the soil produces blue hydrangeas.*

If wine ferments for too long, acetic acid forms. This acid turns the wine into vinegar. Any fruit or vegetable can be fermented to make vinegar.

◀ *Acid tests are useful in distinguishing between some rocks and minerals. When a few drops of hydrochloric acid are placed on limestone, the rock fizzes. This does not happen when the acid is put on dolomite, a rock which may be confused with limestone.*

Strong acids will dissolve most metals, but they do not affect gold. One way of testing whether something is gold or an imitation is to test it with acid. This is the origin of the phrase "to give something the acid test." Gold is dissolved in the laboratory by a mixture of hydrochloric and nitric acids: this is called *aqua regia* (Latin for royal water).

▲ *These acrobats need great skill. They are doing expert stunts on a moving ladder.*

Acids and Health Our bodies need acids to keep healthy. Protein foods such as meat, fish, soybeans, and wheat flour provide *amino acids* that help build body tissue. Humans also need *ascorbic acid* (found in oranges, potatoes, and tomatoes, for example) otherwise they may suffer from a disease called scurvy. Pellagra, a skin complaint, is caused by a lack of *nicotinic acid* in the diet. Liver, bran, and wholewheat are foods containing large amounts of this acid.

■ **LEARN BY DOING**

You can make your own indicator to test for acids and bases. Chop up a few of the outer leaves of a red cabbage. Put them in a pan with enough water to cover them. Boil the water until it turns purple, probably about 20 minutes. Remove the cabbage leaves by straining the liquid into a container.

When the liquid has cooled, put some of it into a jar and add a little lemon juice. The color changes from purple to red. Next, put some of the indicator into another jar. Add a little baking soda. This time the liquid changes to greenish blue. Why?

You are now ready to test some of the liquids around your home to see if they are acid or base. For example, put a drop of liquid soap into some of the indicator. Does it change color? Now add some vinegar to the same liquid. What happens now? Is liquid soap an acid or a base? What happens when a substance you test is neutral? ■

Acids and Bases are Useful A small amount of acid gives flavor to our food. We add vinegar, a mild acid, to pickles, lettuce, and other foods to give them a slightly sour taste.

Acids are used in very many industrial processes. They are used to make other chemicals, for cleaning metals, and to etch (mark) glass and other materials.

FOUR IMPORTANT ACIDS

Sulfuric Acid
Chemical name H_2SO_4
Uses: fertilizers, purifying metals, dyes, medicines
Burns the skin

Hydrochloric Acid
Chemical name HCl
Uses: in chemical plants and laboratories
Burns the skin

Nitric Acid
Chemical name HNO_3
Uses: explosives, medicines, dyes, fertilizers
Burns the skin

Citric Acid
Chemical Name $C_6H_8O_7$
Uses: in the preparation of lemon-flavored drinks
A natural acid in citrus fruits

Bases are useful too. Windows sparkle when washed with water containing ammonia, a common base. Car tires, the pages of this book, and some of the clothes you are wearing were made with the help of bases.

ALSO READ: CHEMISTRY, FIRST AID, POISON, TASTE.

ACNE see SKIN.

ACOUSTICS see SOUND.

ACROBATICS The word *acrobat* comes from two Greek words that mean "one who walks on tip-toes" and "one who climbs high." Persons who can move quickly, perform gymnastics, and keep their balance high above the ground are acrobats. Acrobats were greatly admired in ancient China, Egypt, Greece, and Crete. Tightrope walkers were honored in ancient Rome. At fairs during the Middle Ages, tumblers performed somersaults, back-flips, and other tricks to entertain large groups of people.

Most of us have swung on a rope, or climbed a tree. But just being able to climb or swing does not make someone an acrobat. An acrobat must have strong muscles and good control of them (called *coordination*). He or she must be in top physical condition, and must spend many years training to be an acrobat. A good way to begin acrobatics is to practice routines on a trampoline.

Circus Acrobats The most dangerous and spectacular forms of acrobatics are seen in circuses. *Aerialists*, or high-trapeze artists, have been thrilling audiences for many years. Perhaps you've heard an old song called "The Daring Young Man on the Flying Trapeze." A *trapeze* is a small swinging bar suspended by two ropes. Most trapeze performers use trapezes that are very high above the ground. Performers climb up to their high equipment on a rope ladder. Some performers are so strong they can go up a rope hand-over-hand, without using their legs.

Trapeze artists usually work in teams. An act may begin with the artists standing on two high platforms. One flyer (the "catcher") begins to swing from his trapeze. A partner swings from the opposite platform. The first flyer changes his position on the swinging bar, so that he hangs by his knees, arms outstretched. His partner—with perfect timing—lets go of her trapeze, dives through the air, and is grabbed by the catcher's hands in midair. A third flyer may join in, to do a triple somersault through the air between the other two performers. All of the act is done with split-second timing, and to the sound of gasps from the spellbound audience below.

Acrobats called *tightrope walkers* do more than walk across a rope (actually a heavy wire cable). When they do

▲ *Trampolines are used by both acrobats and gymnasts. Bouncing up and down on a trampoline is good fun and exercise for everyone.*

walk on the rope, they wear special shoes with soft soles. But they also do handstands and somersaults. Some ride bikes and even motorcycles on the narrow cable. A famous acrobat called Blondin tightrope-walked across Niagara Falls blindfolded, on stilts, and carrying a man on his back!

Another kind of acrobatics is performed by *high-wire* artists. One of the most famous high-wire acts, called the "Great Wallendas," performed a spectacular "human pyramid," without a safety net beneath them. Four members of the family balanced on a wire with a long rod placed across their shoulders. Two others stood on that rod with another rod on their shoulders. On the very tip-top stood a lone girl far above the crowd.

Acrobatic Safety Circus acrobats are always trying to develop new acts. Their urge to do new stunts sometimes leads them to try dangerous tricks. Most circuses now have large rope safety nets stretched out beneath the acrobats. If a performer loses his balance or his grip, he falls into the net.

ALSO READ: CIRCUS, GYMNASTICS.

Karl Wallenda was head of the famous family of acrobats until his death in 1978. In July, 1970, he walked across Tallulah Gorge in Georgia, on a wire 750 feet (229 m) above the gorge. He walked the 821-foot (250-m) wire in 20 minutes, stopping twice to stand on his head.

▲ *The Parthenon is the greatest of the temples that stand on the Acropolis at Athens. The Acropolis complex was rebuilt after it was destroyed by Persians in 479* B.C.

Lord Elgin was British ambassador to Greece in the early 1800's. He removed ancient marble sculptures from the Acropolis and sent them to London to prevent their destruction in war. Now called the Elgin marbles, they are in the British Museum.

▼ *The "Porch of the Maidens" on the Erechtheum, another famous temple on the Acropolis.*

ACROPOLIS In the Greek city of Athens stands a hill 500 feet (152 m) high. This hill is the Acropolis. The word "acropolis" means "upper city." The ancient Greeks used hills as forts, because fighting uphill was hard for enemies, and as religious centers. Handsome buildings called *temples* were built on these hills to honor the gods and goddesses of the Greeks. Many cities in ancient Greece had an acropolis, but the most famous one is in Athens.

Over 400 years before Christ, several magnificent marble temples were built on the Athens Acropolis in honor of the goddess Athena. The great gatehouse of the Acropolis, called the *Propylaea*, was the Athenians' favorite building.

The most famous temple is the *Parthenon*, designed by Phidias, one of the most noted architects of all time. The Parthenon is one of the most beautiful buildings ever built. Inside it stood a tall gilded statue of Athena, which was lost long ago.

Another temple, the *Erechtheum*, is known for its Porch of the Maidens. The six maidens are *caryatides*, statues of women that hold up the roof of the porch.

Many parts of the original Acropolis temples were destroyed by time and war. In recent times, those that remain have been restored.

ALSO READ: ATHENS; GODS AND GODDESSES; GREECE, ANCIENT; GREEK ART.

ACTORS AND ACTING Everyone is an actor sometimes. Playing "make-believe" is acting. So is dressing up in old clothes. Trying to get out of doing something unpleasant by saying you are sick is acting, too.

An actor pretends to be someone else. He or she *impersonates a character* (person) in a story or play, usually watched by other people who make up the *audience*. To impersonate means to study the character, or *role*, that an actor will play, and then act in such a way that an audience believes the actor is that character.

No one knows when people first started acting, but it is a very ancient art. It probably began with hunting and victory dances, such as the dances of the American Indians. Many religious rites or events were acted out. Telling a story was most important in these ceremonies.

The History of Acting The Greeks were writing plays and performing them in outdoor theaters by the fourth century B.C. Later, the Romans copied the Greeks. Actors became very important. Many of them did not have to pay taxes or fight wars. Mime, or pantomime, which is acting without speaking, became popular. Mime actors use their bodies and faces, rather than their voices, to tell a story.

Foolish plays produced in Rome made acting less serious. Many actors quit. The Romans then trained slaves to act. But people began to think of acting as a bad thing.

During the Middle Ages in Europe, *minstrels* and *troubadours* (singers and poets) and jugglers wandered from place to place, entertaining people. In some churchyards and marketplaces, actors performed in *miracle* or *mystery plays*, which dealt with saints and Biblical events. In the 1500's, *morality plays*, in which characters stood for good and evil, attracted large audiences.

James Burbage built the first theater in England, in 1576. Many companies of actors were formed during the reign of Elizabeth I. William Shakespeare was a famous playwright and actor of that time. Many people, even the ladies and gentlemen of the royal court, came to the theaters.

The Puritans closed down the theaters in England in 1642, because they thought plays were sinful. But theaters reopened when King Charles II came to the throne in 1660. Plays were popular again by the end of the century. Women began to act on the English stage for the first time. Boys had played women's parts in Shakespeare's time.

Plays have remained popular ever since then. Today, actors and actresses have many opportunities for careers on the stage, in television, and in movies.

Acting in the Theater Some of the greatest actors in theater history are Richard Burbage (James's son), David Garrick, Adrienne Lecouvreur, Sarah Siddons, Henry Irving, Sarah Bernhardt, Laurence Olivier, Eleanora Duse, Katharine Cornell, and the Barrymore family. Many world-famous actors have performed

in New York City, the center of professional theater in the United States. Touring companies, college and high school acting groups, summer theaters, community theaters, and children's theaters are located all over the United States.

An actor uses talent, education, experience, and imagination to create a role for the stage. He must use both his voice and his body when he acts. To be a successful actor, he must study and practice. He must observe other people and understand their emotions. He must learn the *motivations* (reasons) for people's behavior, so that his acting is believable.

Acting in the Movies Many movie actors and actresses are more famous than kings and presidents, because millions of people all over the world watch movies. Hollywood, California, the capital of the movie industry, created the star system. A *star* is an actor or actress who is considered to be an outstanding performer, and who has leading roles in movies. Actors such as Charlie Chaplin, Clark Gable, Elizabeth Taylor, and Dustin Hoffman became world-famous because of their movies.

Working in movies is different

▲ *Marcel Marceau, the French actor, is one of the world's great* mimes. *Mimes are actors who show what they mean by gestures and facial expressions instead of using spoken words.*

Throughout history actors have been treated in different ways. In ancient Greece they enjoyed honors and privileges. In ancient Rome they were once banished from the city!

◄ *Special effects play an important part in modern movies. Actors must learn to work with the technical wizards. This is a scene from* Back to the Future.

▲ *Some children become famous actors. Shirley Temple was a popular child star of the 1930's. She starred in this movie with Gary Cooper.*

▶ *The Marx brothers (Groucho, Chico, Gummo, Harpo, and Zeppo) were Jewish-American comic actors. Groucho, Chico, and Harpo became the most famous. The three are shown here in a scene from their movie* A Day at the Races.

▲ *A scene from the musical* My Fair Lady. *The movie was based on the stage play* Pygmalion *by George Bernard Shaw.*

▶ *Walt Disney (1901-66) with a life-size Mickey Mouse. Disney invented this famous cartoon character.*

from working in the theater. A theater actor performs in a whole play in front of people. In a movie, he works in bits and pieces in front of a camera. He may perform the last scenes first, and weeks later do the first scene. He must sometimes travel to distant places, or go on location, to film some sections of a movie.

Television and Radio Acting for television is somewhat different from stage acting. The television screen is small, so TV actors tend to make much smaller movements and gestures.

Radio actors and comedians were popular in the 1930's and 1940's. Jack Benny, Fred Allen, and Orson Welles were made famous by radio. *Soap operas*, stories that continue from day to day, began on radio, later switching to television. After television arrived, radio lost some of its popular appeal.

Acting Styles There are two basic styles of acting. To be a good actor, it is probably best to combine the two styles. The first style uses *external techniques* alone. An actor uses gestures, movements, and vocal and facial expression to create a believable character. A skillful actor can make his audience feel emotions through his movements and voice, even when he does not feel all the emotion himself. This kind of acting can sometimes seem faked when done by a poor actor.

The second style of acting uses *internal techniques*. The most famous of these techniques is called the *Stanislavski method*, named after the Russian actor and director Konstantin Stanislavski. This is sometimes called "method" acting. Stanislavski taught that an actor can make his part believable only when he really feels the emotions of his character. If an actor is playing an unhappy person, he tries to feel sad himself. An unskilled actor may get careless using this method. He may not speak clearly, or he may not respond properly to another actor's words.

■ **LEARN BY DOING**

With some friends, why not try some acting? One game that is fun is "paper bag theater." Divide the group into two teams. Each group puts into a paper bag five or six things, such as a comb, a handkerchief, a doll, a seashell, and so on. Each group trades its bag with the other. From its bagful of surprises, each group makes up a play using all the items in the bag and then, after

◀ *Big Bird, a character on television's* Sesame Street. *The actor is disguised, but the character is well-loved by children.*

about an hour, presents their play to the other group. You'll be amazed at the plays and the acting started by a few things in a paper bag. ■

Becoming an Actor To become a good actor, a person must train his body, voice, and mind to express what a character is really like. *Mimicry* (imitating) of voices, mannerisms, and movement is good training. Acting in school plays is fun, and useful too. To become a professional actor, the student usually goes to a special school. Many colleges and universities have classes in acting and drama. There are also many acting schools in large cities, such as the Actor's Studio in New York City. While an actor studies his craft, he usually continues to *audition* (try out) for plays or movies, hoping some day he will get an important leading role.

Rewards of Acting Very few actors are successful enough to earn worldwide fame and large sums of money. All actors appreciate awards for their talents. One of the best-known awards is the Academy Award, or *Oscar*. It is presented every year by the Academy of Motion Picture Arts and Sciences, for best performances in movies. The best television actors

win *Emmy* awards presented by the Academy of Television Arts and Sciences. Stage actors are given awards, too. Most famous is the Antoinette Perry Award, called the *Tony*.

ALSO READ: ACADEMY AWARD; DRAMA; MOTION PICTURES; PANTOMIME; SHAKESPEARE, WILLIAM; THEATER.

ACUPUNCTURE Sticking needles into people can actually relieve pain, not make it worse! This was discovered many hundreds of years ago by the Chinese. The medical treatment based on this principle is called *acupuncture*.

In ancient China, as in other countries, doctors believed that illness was caused by some kind of upset in the natural balance of the human body. Doctors in medieval Europe thought they could cure this balance by "bleeding," or draining off some of the sick person's blood. In China, doctors believed that by sticking needles into certain points on the body, natural health could be restored.

Ancient drawings show the points on the body where needles may be inserted. Western doctors have watched in surprise as Chinese surgeons operated on a patient without

Medical students in China are taught ancient techniques, such as acupuncture, alongside modern medicine. Western observers have been startled to watch operations carried out on patients who, instead of being given a pain-killing anesthetic, had been prepared for surgery by the insertion of acupuncture needles. The patients appeared perfectly happy to be needled in this way.

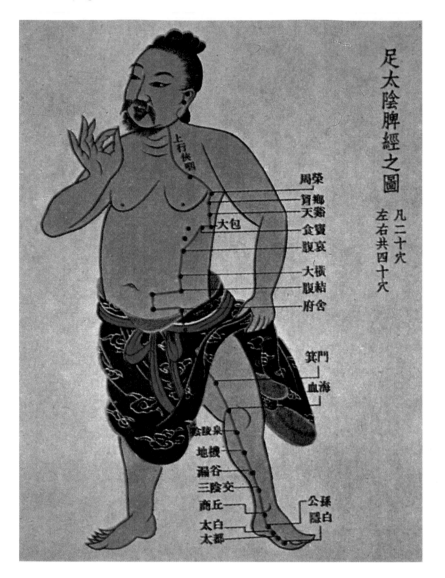

足太陰脾經之圖

凡二十穴

左右共四十穴

周榮
胸鄉
天谿
食竇
腹哀
大橫
腹結
府舍
上行候喉
大包
箕門
血海
陰陵泉
地機
漏谷
三陰交
商丘
太白
太都
公孫
隱白

▲ *Acupuncture—the practice of inserting needles in the body—has been used in Chinese medicine for thousands of years. This picture shows some of the points on the body where the needles are placed.*

anesthetics. Instead, the patient had needles stuck into her wrists. She remained awake during the operation, but apparently felt no pain.

How acupuncture works is a mystery that not even the Chinese fully understand. It is said to help patients suffering from malaria fever, narcotics addiction, rheumatism, arthritis, back pain, and headaches. The needles used are up to 9 inches (24 cm) long. Acupuncture is now practiced in other countries outside China.

ALSO READ: ANESTHETIC, CHINA, MEDICINE.

ADAMS, JOHN (1735–1826)
The second president of the United States was John Adams. His family were farmers in Massachusetts, where his great-great-grandfather, Henry Adams, had settled in 1636.

John Adams first studied at Harvard College to become a minister. But he decided to study law instead. He became known throughout Massachusetts as an honest, courageous, and able lawyer. He was a leader in the American colonies' fight for independence from Great Britain. In 1774, he went to the First Continental Congress. He signed the Declaration of Independence at the Second Congress, in 1776. He worked hard to convince the colonies to accept the Declaration. Adams went to France and the Netherlands during the American Revolution, to urge those countries to support the colonists. John Adams, Benjamin Franklin, and John Jay worked on the peace treaty with Britain, in 1783. Adams served as George Washington's Vice President after the Revolution. He was a leader of the political group known as the Federalists.

When Adams became President in 1797, France was at war with several European countries. U.S. ships were being attacked at sea. Many Americans, led by Thomas Jefferson, supported the French Revolution; they wanted to give aid to France. The Federalists, however, led by Alexander Hamilton, wanted to restore the French king and urged a war against France. Adams himself wanted to keep the United States neutral.

U.S. diplomats were sent to France to work out a peace treaty. Negotiations ended in anger after three French diplomats tried to bribe the U.S. (in what is known as the XYZ Affair). French and U.S. warships fought several battles until President Adams and French Foreign Minister Talleyrand signed a treaty in 1799.

Although the treaty kept the U.S. out of war, it made President Adams very unpopular, especially with the Federalists. Another cause of his un-

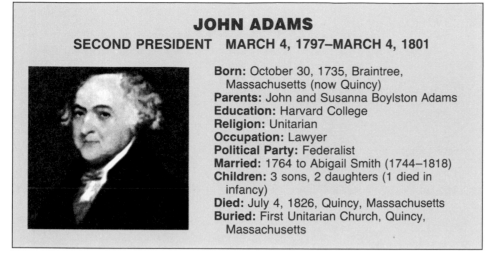

JOHN ADAMS
SECOND PRESIDENT   MARCH 4, 1797–MARCH 4, 1801

Born: October 30, 1735, Braintree, Massachusetts (now Quincy)
Parents: John and Susanna Boylston Adams
Education: Harvard College
Religion: Unitarian
Occupation: Lawyer
Political Party: Federalist
Married: 1764 to Abigail Smith (1744–1818)
Children: 3 sons, 2 daughters (1 died in infancy)
Died: July 4, 1826, Quincy, Massachusetts
Buried: First Unitarian Church, Quincy, Massachusetts

popularity was his support of the Alien and Sedition Acts. Adams was not reelected, and Thomas Jefferson became President in 1801.

John Adams was one of the most famous members of a noted American family. His second cousin was Samuel Adams, a leader of the American Revolution and, with John, one of those who signed the Declaration of Independence. Another interesting family member was John's wife, Abigail (1744–1818), probably the best-informed woman of her day. She is remembered for the intelligent, amusing letters she wrote to her husband during his stay in Europe. You can find out more about Abigail by reading her letters. The eldest son of John and Abigail, John Quincy Adams, was the sixth President of the United States.

ALSO READ: ADAMS, JOHN QUINCY; ADAMS, SAMUEL; CONTINENTAL CONGRESS; HAMILTON, ALEXANDER; JEFFERSON, THOMAS; PRESIDENCY.

ADAMS, JOHN QUINCY (1767–1848) The American Revolution began when John Quincy Adams was eight. He and his mother watched the Battle of Bunker Hill from a nearby field. Later, he went with his father, John Adams, on a government mission to France. They sailed safely through a line of enemy British ships, but they were shipwrecked in Spain. Riding mules, they took three months to reach Paris. When he was 14, John Quincy was an aide to the first U.S. diplomat to go to Russia. He later went with his father to the peace treaty conferences between the United States and Great Britain at the end of the American Revolution. John Quincy Adams was an experienced traveler and diplomat by the time he graduated from Harvard College in 1787.

Adams served as an ambassador for President George Washington, and then for his own father, who followed Washington as President. Then John Quincy, too, entered politics. He was elected to the Senate in 1803. But he angered his own political party, the Federalists, because he did not always vote the way they wanted him to. After five years, they elected a new Senator. President Madison then asked Adams to become a diplomat again and sent him to Europe. President Monroe made Adams his Secretary of State in 1817. Adams acquired Florida from Spain for the U.S. and helped write the Monroe Doctrine.

In the Presidential election of 1824, Adams was one of four candidates. Andrew Jackson received the most popular votes, but not enough electoral votes to win. The House of Representatives had to decide who

▲ *This is how the U.S. Capitol looked when John Adams was President. The building was not finished, and the city of Washington, D.C., was hardly begun.*

When John Adams became President in 1797 the population of the United States was only 4,900,000. He was the first President to live in the White House.

When John Quincy Adams was president, the Erie Canal was completed (1825). It linked New York with the Great Lakes and the boat trip took eight days.

Also during his presidency, in 1828, Webster's Dictionary was first published. It gained fame as the best English dictionary of its time.

JOHN QUINCY ADAMS
SIXTH PRESIDENT   MARCH 4, 1825–MARCH 4, 1829

Born: July 11, 1767, Braintree (now Quincy), Massachusetts
Parents: John and Abigail Smith Adams
Education: University of Leyden, the Netherlands; Harvard College
Religion: Unitarian
Occupation: Lawyer
Political Party: Federalist, then National Republican
Married: 1797 to Louisa Catherine Johnson (1775–1852)
Children: 3 sons, 1 daughter (died in infancy)
Died: February 23, 1848, Washington, D.C.
Buried: First Unitarian Church, Quincy, Massachusetts

would be President, and they picked Adams. Jackson's supporters in Congress argued constantly with President Adams. He had good ideas, but they were not accepted, because he was not popular. In 1828, Andrew Jackson was elected President.

Adams went back to Washington in 1831, this time as a congressman from Massachusetts. He served for 17 years. He believed that slavery was wrong and should be stopped. He spoke about it so often that slave owners called him the "Madman from Massachusetts." In 1848, he collapsed in the House of Representatives, and he died two days later.

ALSO READ: ADAMS, JOHN; JACKSON, ANDREW; PRESIDENCY.

ADAMS, SAMUEL (1722–1803)
"A hot-headed radical!" "An arch traitor!" These were just two of many names the British called Samuel Adams of Boston in the years before the American Revolution. Sam went to Harvard College, like his younger cousin John Adams. Also, like John, Sam never stopped fighting for the independence of the American colonies from Great Britain.

Samuel Adams constantly gave speeches to tell the colonies they had

▲ *Samuel Adams, American patriot and Revolutionary leader.*

to be free from British rule. He urged the colonists to protest the Stamp Act and other examples of "taxation without representation." He helped organize groups of rebels, such as the Sons of Liberty. He led the Boston Tea Party. Adams and his friend Patrick Henry were both delegates to the Continental Congress. They urged the other delegates to demand immediate independence for the colonies. Samuel Adams voted for and signed the Declaration of Independence.

Adams served in the Continental Congress during the Revolution. Then he returned to Boston. He was governor of Massachusetts from 1794 to 1797. In American history, Samuel Adams is remembered as an important leader of the American Revolution.

ALSO READ: ADAMS, JOHN; BOSTON TEA PARTY; CONTINENTAL CONGRESS; DECLARATION OF INDEPENDENCE.

ADAPTATION   see EVOLUTION.

ADDAMS, JANE (1860–1935)
"She belongs to all people." "She was everybody's friend." Jane Addams earned this praise from a lifetime spent helping people. She worked for

the poor, for immigrants and minority groups, for women and children.

Born in Cedarville, Illinois, Jane graduated from nearby Rockford College. She had been born with a badly curved back. She wanted to be a doctor, but her poor health kept her from finishing medical school.

Her family sent her to Europe to recover. In London she visited a *settlement house*—a gathering place and education center for poor people. She decided to start such a place for the poor of Chicago. Hull House was the result. Jane and her friend, Ellen Starr, worked hard at Hull House. They set up various programs, from day nurseries to adult evening classes. Hull House became a model for the rest of the nation.

Jane Addams called social work the profession of helping people in need—in need of food, clothing, housing, education, work, or play. She helped women win the right to vote. Her work for world peace won her the Nobel Peace Prize when she was 71.

ALSO READ: SOCIAL WORK.

ADDICTION Using some drugs for a long time can make people need to keep on taking them. This need is called *addiction*. The drug users, or *addicts*, become addicted when they take habit-forming drugs often, for a long time. Their need for a drug is called a *habit*. Their habit makes them take larger and larger amounts of the drugs. People can become addicted to other habits, like drinking alcohol or smoking.

There are different kinds of addictive drugs. Some drugs, such as sleeping pills and "pep pills," act on the body's central nervous system. The addicts think they need such drugs, especially during times of stress. This need of the mind is called *mental dependence*. Other drugs, called *narcotics*, set up such a need that the

addicts' bodies cannot do without them. This kind of need is called *physical dependence*. If the drugs are taken away from an addict with a physical dependence, he or she experiences *withdrawal* symptoms. One of these symptoms is intense pain. People who use *heroin* and then stop must suffer through withdrawal. Heroin has medical usages, but it is so addictive that it is never prescribed.

Many drugs that cause physical or mental dependence are dangerous and illegal. There are four main kinds of drugs. (1) *Pain killers*, such as opium, morphine, and codeine, are given to patients by doctors to stop severe pain. But if people take these drugs over a period of time, they develop physical dependence. (2) *Depressants* slow, or relax, the central nervous system. Sleeping pills (*sedatives*) are depressants. (3) Other drugs called *stimulants* pep up the central nervous system. These include *amphetamines*, which are called "speed." (4) *Hallucinogens* are the fourth main kind of drug. They are drugs that make a person see colors and objects and hear sounds that are not really there. Marijuana is an hallucinogen. LSD (lysergic acid diethylamide) and similar chemicals are the strongest and most dangerous hallucinogens. Drug users usually do not become physically addicted to hallucinogens, but the drugs often cause mental dependence, and may lead users to try narcotics.

Drug addiction and misuse have grown greatly in recent years. Treatment of addicts has become a big community problem. Addicts hurt themselves by using drugs; they may die. Addicts may turn to crime to raise money to buy drugs.

Most ways of treating addicts start by *withdrawing* the drug. People addicted to "hard" drugs, such as heroin or cocaine, usually stay in treatment centers, to stop them from getting new supplies of drugs and to have help available during the pain of

▲ *Jane Addams, social reformer. She worked to improve life for the poor and sick, especially women and children.*

▲ *Hull House, where Jane Addams worked to give people a better life. It is now part of the University of Illinois at Chicago.*

withdrawal. Many scientists are trying to develop safe drugs that can be given as substitutes for hard drugs during the withdrawal period. It is very, very difficult to break an addiction and not many addicts are successful. Those who get past the withdrawal period need help for a long time after this.

The best way to prevent addiction is to keep people from getting harmful drugs, except when a doctor *prescribes* (gives) them. Mental health and drug-education programs give information on drugs to help young people avoid misusing drugs.

ALSO READ: DRUG ABUSE, NARCOTICS.

ADDITION   see ARITHMETIC.

ADENAUER, KONRAD (1876–1967) Konrad Adenauer was the first Chancellor (chief minister of state) of West Germany. He was elected in 1949—at age 73—when Germany was divided and suffering from its defeat in World War II. Adenauer helped rebuild his war-torn country. Today, West Germany is one of the major industrial nations in the world.

Adenauer was born in Cologne, Germany. He became a lawyer and entered politics when he was 30 years old. He was elected mayor of Cologne in 1917. He remained active in politics until 1933, when Adolf Hitler's Nazi party took over Germany. The Nazis removed Adenauer from office because he spoke up against them. They imprisoned him twice during the war.

After World War II, Adenauer organized a new political party, the Christian Democratic Union. He also helped write a constitution for West Germany before he was elected Chancellor. As Chancellor, he helped improve West Germany's relations with the United States and other European

nations. Adenauer signed a "Treaty of Cooperation" with France in 1963. This treaty helped end the long hostility between Germany and France. Konrad Adenauer retired in 1963, knowing that West Germany was a strong and respected nation.

ALSO READ: GERMAN HISTORY; HITLER, ADOLF; WORLD WAR II.

ADENOIDS   see BREATHING.

ADJECTIVE   see PARTS OF SPEECH.

ADOLESCENCE Boys and girls usually look forward to becoming teenagers. These particular years of growing up are called *adolescence*, which is a time of many changes. The changes usually begin to take place in girls 10 to 13 and in boys 11 to 14. The changes of adolescence go on for several years.

Physical Changes The adolescent's body changes in many ways. Girls are turning into women and boys into men. Hair begins to grow on various parts of the body. Girls' hips become rounder and their breasts develop. Boys' voices deepen, and their muscles grow larger. In both girls and boys the sexual organs mature. These changes are part of *puberty*, the stage of growing up when people become physically able to reproduce.

At first, it seems that girls are growing faster than boys of the same age. But boys soon catch up and then become taller and heavier than most of the girls. Some teenagers start growing very fast and then slow down. Others develop slowly at first and later speed up.

Because so many changes are taking place in the body, adolescents often are very tired and need extra sleep. Other times, they seem to have a great deal of energy. Their bodies

▲ *Konrad Adenauer helped rebuild his country as West German Chancellor from 1949 to 1963.*

The German people fondly called Konrad Adenauer *Der Alte*, "the old one." He did much of his best work in his 70's.

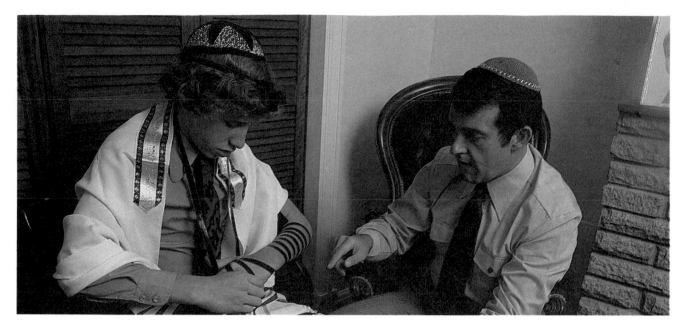

▲ *Adolescence is a time of preparation for adulthood. This Jewish boy is being prepared for his bar mitzvah.*

are sometimes changing so fast that they become very clumsy. They may be embarrassed because they develop pimples on their faces.

But it helps the teenager to know that his or her friends are also going through these changes. Adolescence is a necessary part of growing up to become mature adult men and women.

Changes in Feelings   Just as a small child gives up his wagon and blocks for two-wheelers and mystery books, adolescents' interests change, too. Boys lose interest in their bicycles and look forward to driving cars. Girls no longer want to spend time making doll clothes, but become interested in their own clothes instead. Both boys and girls become interested in each other. They spend a lot of time together and learn many things about getting along with the opposite sex, which will help them later when they want to marry.

Adolescents' feelings may be confused because they are no longer a child but are not quite a grown-up. Sometimes they cry very easily and other times they act as though nothing can hurt them. Parents who are understanding (and remember their own adolescence) can help make

things easier. Teenagers still need the love and help of their parents, but of a different kind. They need support and encouragement, but they must also be free to make many decisions themselves, even though some will be mistakes.

Adolescence is a time of adventure. Teenagers begin thinking about what kind of work they want to do as adults. They also begin preparing for this work in school. They make plans about whether or not to go to college. Sometimes they take part-time jobs. They learn to do more and more things for themselves, so that they do not have to depend so much on their parents. They want to think out answers for themselves. Many adolescents are very concerned with problems in their community and their nation, such as pollution and war and discrimination. They are well on their way to becoming responsible adults.

ALSO READ: AGING, GROWTH, HUMAN BODY, REPRODUCTION.

ADOPTION   Some children have no family because their parents are dead or are too sick or have too many problems to take care of them. Men and women who do not have children

It is estimated that 2 out of every 100 children in the United States are adopted. About half of these children are adopted by relatives.

Adoption is mentioned in many old legends and stories. The Bible tells how Moses was adopted by Pharaoh's daughter.

of their own may *adopt* children who have no families. To adopt means to become the legal parent of someone else's child. Often, if a person marries someone with children, he or she adopts those children. Sometimes a mother allows her new baby to be adopted because she cannot make a good home for the child and she wants him to be happy.

Adoption agencies have the job of making sure that the people who want to adopt children can give the children good, loving homes. These agencies try to keep brothers and sisters together.

A child cannot be adopted until an agency learns all about the child and the people who want to adopt him. The child usually lives with his new family for a while. If the agency thinks that the child will be happy with his new family, a court makes the adoption legal. Then the child really becomes part of his new family. His last name is changed to theirs. And his natural parents—those to whom he was born—cannot take him from his adopted family.

Adoption can ensure good homes for children who need special love and understanding. Sometimes these are older children, or children who have physical or mental problems.

ALSO READ: CHILD CARE.

▼ *The Adriatic Sea is between Italy and Yugoslavia. This sea has been a route for travelers through many centuries.*

ADRIATIC SEA Italy is shaped like a boot sticking southward into the Mediterranean Sea. The Adriatic Sea lies along the back of the boot. The Adriatic is actually a gulf of the Mediterranean Sea. (See the map with the article on EUROPE.)

The Adriatic was named after the ancient town of Adria, once a major Roman port. Roman sailing ships, bulging with cargo, crisscrossed the Adriatic. Many vessels sailed through the Strait of Otranto into the open waters of the Mediterranean and beyond. The place where Adria stood now lies 15 miles (24 km) from the sea, because mud has piled up at the mouth of the Po River and pushed back the sea.

The Adriatic's Italian coastline is low-lying and has few harbors. On the eastern side of the sea, the coasts of Yugoslavia and Albania have steep sides and good harbors. Many islands are near the Yugoslav shore. Wealthy Romans once built summer homes along this rugged coast. Today, there are tourist hotels and vineyards. Fishermen sail from the harbors to cast nets into the Adriatic for sardines. Venice, the city of canals, lies at the top of the Adriatic.

ALSO READ: MEDITERRANEAN SEA; ROME, ANCIENT; VENICE; YUGOSLAVIA.

ADVERB see PARTS OF SPEECH.

ADVERTISING Advertising is the business of trying to convince a *consumer* what to buy. A consumer is a buyer of products or a user of services. Business and industry provide more products and services than any one person can ever use.

One kind of product may be made by several different companies. So each company uses its own special name for a product. That special name is called the company's *brand*

name. No other company can use that name. Coca-Cola and Kleenex are brand names.

Ads Are Persuaders Advertising gives useful information about which products to buy. But modern advertising does more than give news about products and services. Today's advertisements, or ads, try to get consumers to buy certain brands. Writers of advertising are so skillful they can sometimes persuade a consumer to wear a certain kind of clothing, eat a special kind of cereal, or see a movie. Consumers might never even want a product if they did not see or hear advertisements for it.

For example, you probably do not need the newest cereal in the supermarket. There are probably many cereal brands on your kitchen shelves. You may not have space on a shelf for another. But if you see ads about a new cereal that is extra-tasty and has a free prize in the box, you may want it.

Advertising must get attention. To be effective, it must be exciting, entertaining, or provide some pleasure. The secret of writing good advertising *copy* is to offer a good idea as well as a product. The idea is what the ad is really selling. One example is an ad that says eating a certain cereal will make a person do well in sports. That cereal brand may sell better if consumers think it offers strength and energy.

■ LEARN BY DOING

Suppose you are running a lemonade stand in your neighborhood. How would you advertise it?

First, you could decorate your stand with different colors of crepe paper. Next, you could paint a large, bright sign, so that people notice you.

Maybe you could write some handout posters. Your copy should say something about the lemonade to make people want to buy it. Think of how good a glass of lemonade is on a hot summer day.

If someone else has a lemonade stand on your block, he may take business away from you. If this happens, you can offer something he does not have, to win back business. You can advertise that your lemonade is made with fresh lemons instead of with a frozen mix. Many *advertisers* offer other things along with the products they are trying to sell, such as prizes or trading stamps. Perhaps you could find something to give away with your lemonade. How about a special offer? ■

The Media A communications *medium* is a means of carrying information to an audience. The plural form of medium is *media*. Some examples of media are television, films, newspapers, magazines, and radio. Advertising uses nearly all media.

▲ *An 1853 poster advertising buses. Before magazines and television, posters were important advertising media.*

▼ *A French advertisement from around 1900 for various forms of wheeled transport.*

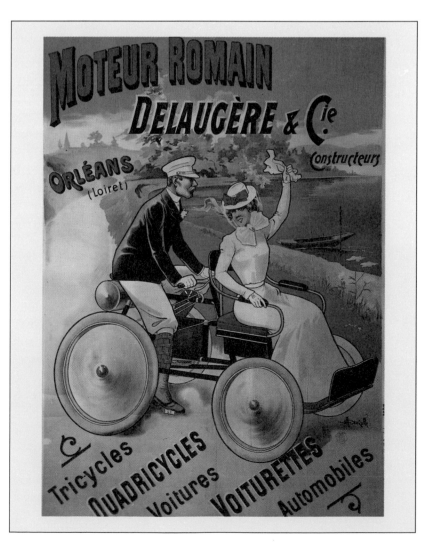

▲ *Years ago big wooden Indians stood outside cigar stores to advertise tobacco. The models were carved and painted, and often held cigars in their hands.*

The red-and-white striped pole outside a barber shop was an old form of advertising. It was colored red (for blood) and white (for bandages) as a reminder of the days when the local barber was also the doctor and surgeon.

▲ *Advertisements can make a product well-known in many countries and in many languages.*

Many ads can be found in the *print* media, such as newspapers, magazines, catalogs, telephone directories, posters, and billboards. Newspapers and magazines depend on advertising to pay the cost of printing them. Payments that newspapers and magazines get from advertisers give publishers enough money to sell their newspapers or magazines for much less than it costs to print and mail them. Successful magazines make most of their money from the advertising they carry. Some newspapers and magazines have so much advertising that they can be given away, not sold.

Ads go wherever people can see them. *Outdoor advertising* is mounted above the windows and doors of buses and subways. Ads are sometimes painted on sides of buildings. Big ads made of electric lights flash on and off at night in the downtown parts of cities.

Direct mail advertising uses letters and colorful brochures mailed to people's homes. The letters or brochures may ask people to subscribe to magazines, give money to charity, order books through the mail, or attend a special sale.

Radio and television ads, called *commercials*, probably reach the most people. A special television program may be viewed by 100 million or more persons. Advertising on TV is expensive. For example, a few seconds ad time on a TV network costs thousands of dollars. But if 50 million persons see that ad, the advertiser pays only a tiny cost for each person who sees it. Because TV ads, especially at peak viewing times, are so expensive, not all companies can afford to advertise on TV.

When Did Advertising Begin?
Town criers in ancient Greece called out what could be bought in the local marketplaces. Newsboys still hawk (advertise by shouting) papers in big cities as they walk down the street.

The earliest billboards were in ancient Egypt. The Egyptians carved announcements on tall stones called *stelae*. Ads were first printed in 1480. William Caxton, one of the first English printers, nailed printed papers on church doors to advertise a religious book he was selling.

Many different newspapers and magazines appeared in Europe and America in the 1800's. Britain took the lead in advertising in the print media. But, by the 1860's, American manufacturers had seized the new opportunities offered by advertising. Special *advertising agencies* were set up to create ads.

Advertising agencies grew into big businesses with the coming of radio and television in the 20th century. An agency provides advertising to the media for anyone with a product or service to sell. In advertising, a customer is called a *client*. A client can be one person or a huge company. A client has an *account* with an ad agency. An account includes the entire job of producing the client's ads and getting them into the media. An agency and a client agree on the media that will carry the ads. A team then goes to work. Most ads—even television ads—need an illustrator, a copy writer, a designer, and often a photographer. Audio and video tapes are needed for radio and television ads.

ALSO READ: CONSUMER PROTECTION, PATENTS AND COPYRIGHTS, PROPAGANDA, PUBLIC RELATIONS.

AEGEAN SEA Lying between Greece and Turkey is the Aegean Sea. It is an arm of the Mediterranean Sea. Crete, the largest island belonging to Greece, lies at its south end. About 400 other islands are also in the Aegean. (See the map with the article on EUROPE.)

The Aegean Sea covers more than 69,000 square miles (178,700 square km). At its widest point, it is about

◀ *The Aegean Sea has an ancient history and a lively present. Its warm climate and beautiful island scenery attract many tourists.*

200 miles (322 km) across, and 400 miles (644 km) long. Most of the Aegean islands belong to Greece, and many are "dead" volcanoes. Tourists come to enjoy the historical sites, the warm sun and sandy beaches, while the local people fish in the sea, and grow grapes to produce wine and raisins.

The Aegean was the center of a rich ancient civilization, that lasted from about 3000 B.C. to 1200 B.C. The Minoans (named after the legendary King Minos of Crete) and the Myceneans were peoples of the Aegean region. Great cities were built around the sea's natural harbors. Trading ships carried bronze and gold. Adventurers went in search of fortunes. Many stories were told by the Greeks about these exciting times. The beautiful temples and palaces of the Aegean islands, some of which are still standing, remind visitors of this lost world.

ALSO READ: ANCIENT CIVILIZATIONS; GREECE, ANCIENT; MEDITERRANEAN SEA.

AEROSOL A fluffy white cloud in the blue sky overhead is one kind of aerosol. The unpleasant smog that stings your eyes and makes breathing difficult is an aerosol, too. An aerosol is a scattering of very tiny droplets of liquid, or bits of a solid, in a gas.

Clouds are droplets of water hanging in air. *Fog* is a cloud at ground level. Solid bits of carbon or ash in air form an aerosol called *smoke*. If smoke is mixed with fog, *smog* is the result. Clouds and smog are examples of natural aerosols.

Whipping cream, paint, and insect sprays can be bought in *aerosol cans*. A non-poisonous gas, called a *propellant*, is put in the can under such high pressure that it turns to a liquid. A useful product, such as paint, is mixed with the propellant. When a button on the can is pushed, the propellant sprays out, carrying the paint with it. The propellant turns back to gas and evaporates in the air.

Scientists now agree that aerosols are slowly helping to destroy the ozone layer—a layer of gas about 12 miles (20 km) above Earth. It is this layer that protects us from most of the sun's dangerous ultraviolet rays. Chemicals named chlorofluorocarbons, or CFC's, used as propellants in most aerosols, drift slowly up in the air and begin to make holes in the layer.

Some aerosol manufacturers are producing cans in which the propellant is a more harmless gas. CFC gas is also used in refrigeration systems and to make the bubbles in foam plastic.

ALSO READ: AIR POLLUTION, ATMOSPHERE, CLOUD, GAS, OZONE LAYER.

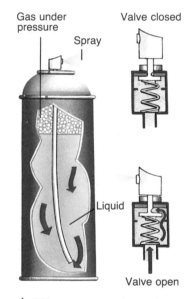

▲ *When you press down the nozzle of an aerosol can, it releases a spray of fine drops of liquid. Gas under pressure forces the liquid out of the nozzle.*

▲ *The U.S. Saturn 5 rocket blasting off. This multi-stage launcher was used by NASA for the Apollo moonlanding program.*

AEROSPACE The beginning of the Space Age in the 1950's added a new word to our vocabularies—*aerospace*. Scientists saw that the Earth's atmosphere and outer space together can be seen as one vast realm that includes everything from the surface of the Earth outward. This realm is *aerospace*.

The word also means the science of all flight within the realm of aerospace. This includes *aeronautics*, the science of navigating through air, and *astronautics*, the science of navigating through space. Craft that move through the air are *aircraft*. Craft that move through space are *spacecraft*. The Space Shuttle can be rocketed into space, and glide back to Earth. Soon there will be true *aerospace craft*, which will fly like airplanes in the atmosphere and like rocket-driven spacecraft in space. One of the achievements of aerospace science is the study of the planets at close range by spacecraft.

The human desire to explore space led to the aerospace industry. Hundreds of thousands of new jobs were created. It takes huge amounts of energy to launch craft into space. So engineers and technicians learned how to make large parts small—this is called "miniaturization"—so they could be used in space travel. Experts found how to guide robot spacecraft to faraway planets, and how to keep human beings alive in space. They learned how to put artificial satellites in orbit around the Earth.

Aerospace technology has become part of everyday life. Television programs from other continents, improved telephone calls across the ocean, more accurate maps, and better weather forecasts are some of the results. The space photographs we now see of Earth would not have been possible before aerospace research.

ALSO READ: ASTRONOMY, AVIATION, SPACE, SPACE RESEARCH, SPACE TRAVEL.

AESCHYLUS (525–456 B.C.) Aeschylus was the first great Greek writer of tragedy. He lived most of his life in Athens. As a young man, he helped defeat the Persians at the Battle of Marathon in 490 B.C.

Aeschylus wrote about 90 plays, of which only seven survive in full to-

▶ *Skylab was a manned science laboratory in space. Launched in 1974, it was visited by three crews of U.S. astronauts who carried out experiments in orbit.*

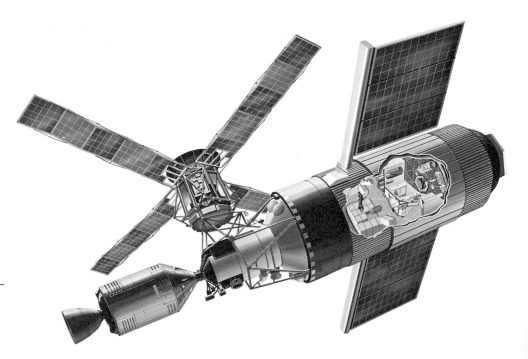

day. Many people consider them the first real tragic dramas in Western culture. Before his time, tragedies consisted of one actor who responded to questions from a chorus. Aeschylus added an actor, and later a third actor. (Though only two or three actors and the chorus were on the stage at one time, an actor sometimes took more than one role.) Also, Aeschylus instilled more life into the various roles and relationships between characters. He added costumes and decorated his stage scenery.

Today, his plays may seem slow and cumbersome to many, but they are filled with deep thoughts about human life. Some say that only William Shakespeare can rival him in richness of language and wisdom.

One of Aeschylus's better known plays is *The Persians*, which praises the Athenian victory over the Persians at the Battle of Salamis in 480 B.C. *Prometheus Bound* attacks the gods for their harsh treatment of man. Aeschylus's greatest work is the trilogy (three plays forming one drama) called the *Oresteia*. It is made up of *Agamemnon*, *The Libation Bearers*, and *The Eumenides*. In the *Oresteia*, Aeschylus deals with the importance of human suffering and the meaning of justice.

After his death, Aeschylus was honored at Athens by having his plays performed repeatedly.

ALSO READ: DRAMA; GREECE, ANCIENT.

AESOP (about 620–562 B.C.) A marvelous storyteller named Aesop lived long ago in Greece. Very little is known about him except that he was a young slave on the island of Samos. Legend says that he was an ugly man, perhaps deformed. But he had a brilliant mind, and he enjoyed telling stories in which animals acted like human beings. Each tale taught people a lesson. These tales are called *fables*.

One legend tells that Aesop was freed from slavery. He was sent to divide money among the people of Delphi, a Greek city. But he found that they were dishonest, and he refused to give them the money. The angry people of Delphi threw Aesop over a cliff to his death.

In those days, stories were shared mostly by word of mouth. Aesop's stories were not written down until at

least 200 years after he died. Since then, they have been translated from Greek into almost every language in the world.

Many people have laughed at Aesop's fable of the race between the slow, patient tortoise and the swift, bragging hare. Perhaps you know the stories about the goose that laid the golden egg, the grasshopper and the ant, or the lion and the mouse. These are just four of *Aesop's Fables*, some of the best-loved stories of all time.

ALSO READ: FABLE.

AFGHANISTAN The land-locked mountain republic of Afghanistan is at the crossroads of Asia, surrounded by the nations of Iran, the Soviet Union, Pakistan, and China. Afghanistan's location has made it important throughout history. Main trade routes run through it, connecting Asia with the Western World. (See the map with the article on ASIA.) In early times, the Persians, Greeks, Arabs, and Mongols conquered the region. Tribal revolts and political assassinations have often disrupted Afghanistan. This helped bring about

▲ *In Aesop's fable of the hare and the tortoise, the slow-but-sure tortoise wins a race with the boastful hare.*

▲ *Aesop's shrewd tales may have earned him his freedom from slavery.*

Legend has it that Aeschylus was killed by a turtle that an eagle dropped while flying over his head. The eagle mistook Aeschylus's bald head for a rock!

41

AFGHANISTAN

Capital City: Kabul (1,036,000 people).
Area: 250,018 square miles (647,497,000 sq. km).
Population: 14,000,000.
Government: Republic.
Natural Resources: Natural gas, some coal, iron ore, and other minerals.
Export Products: Natural gas, cotton, karakul sheepskins, fruit.
Unit of Money: Afghani.
Official Language: Pashtu, Dari.

▲ *The largest statue of Buddha stands near the town of Bamian. This is in the north of Afghanistan.*

It comes as a surprise to most people to learn that Africa is almost as wide as it is long. From north to south it measures 4,400 miles (7,080 km) and from east to west 3,750 miles (6,035 km). The average height of the African continent is 2,460 feet (750 m) above sea level.

the country's troubled present, with a civil war between Soviet-backed government forces and rebels seeking to end outside interference in Afghanistan.

Afghanistan is about the size of Texas. No part of Afghanistan touches a sea. The high Hindu Kush Mountains separate Afghanistan into two sections. Nomads roam the rough mountain country, herding livestock. The Karakul lamb is one of the animals the nomads raise. The curly black Karakul fur is exported, to be made into Persian lamb coats. The low, dry land south of the mountains is a farm region where farmers use river water from the highlands to irrigate crops.

Afghanistan's ancient capital, Kabul, lies on the banks of the Kabul River. Kabul has wide modern streets through which automobiles travel. But the old part of Kabul has unpaved, narrow streets surrounded by high walls of mud-brick houses. Merchants sell fruits, nuts, spices, furs, and jewels in outdoor bazaars (marketplaces).

Transportation beyond the cities is poor in Afghanistan. There are no railroads and few paved roads. People cross the mountains only on foot or on animals. Camel caravans carry goods along rocky roads and through steep mountain passes, such as the famous Khyber Pass. Alexander the Great conquered Afghanistan about 330

B.C., and led his armies through the Khyber Pass to India.

The Afghan people did not know the ways of the outside world for hundreds of years. Most Afghans live far from cities in small, walled villages. Very few nomads or villagers can read or write. Most Afghans still strictly obey the old laws of Islam. Some tribespeople claim they are descended from the Mongol warriors of Genghis Khan.

Afghanistan was a kingdom until 1973, when military forces overthrew the king, Zahir Shah, and set up a republic. In 1978 the republican government, which had begun a democratic reform program, was itself overthrown by pro-Communist forces. The country's new leader, Babrak Karmal, was backed by the Soviets. But there was resistance to the government from tribespeople, and civil war broke out. The U.S. ambassador was killed.

In 1979 Soviet troops entered Afghanistan to prop up the Karmal government. Soviet tanks and helicopter gunships attacked Afghan villages. In 1988, the Soviet Union began to withdraw their troops. During the nine years of conflict, Afghanistan's population shrank by as much as one-third. At least four million people fled to Pakistan or Iran, and up to one million were killed.

ALSO READ: ASIA.

AFRICA Africa is a giant continent, more than three times bigger than the United States. Africa is divided in two by the equator, so the continent is partly in the Northern Hemisphere and partly in the Southern Hemisphere. A narrow bridge of land in the northeast connects Africa to the Sinai Peninsula of Asia. The rest of the continent is surrounded by water. The Mediterranean Sea separates Africa from Europe to the north. The Atlantic Ocean is to the west, and the Red Sea, the Gulf of Aden, and the Indian Ocean are to the east. Several islands—including one of the world's largest, Madagascar—lie off the African mainland.

The Land People used to imagine that most of Africa was a steaming jungle of twisted vines and tangled bushes. Jungles are actually found only in a small part of central Africa. The rest of the continent is mainly desert and grassland. Tropical forests and woodlands occupy about one-fifth of the total area of Africa. The various land regions are distributed over a great *plateau* (a high, fairly level land mass). The plateau rises sharply from the low coastal plains and stretches across most of the continent.

The largest desert in the world—the Sahara—is the main feature of the northern plateau. Two smaller deserts, the Kalahari and the Namib, are in the southern plateau. The deserts are mostly dry and barren, although the Sahara has a few green spots, called oases, where date palms and cereals grow. The rain forests of central Africa, near the equator, are just the opposite. These moist tropical lands are thick with fruit trees, oil palms, and hardwood trees such as ebony and mahogany. The trees often grow so high and thick that sunlight can barely reach the ground.

Between the desert regions and the rain forests are *savannas*—lonely stretches of grassland with scattered trees and shrubs. These lands make up almost half the area of Africa. The dry savannas near the deserts have short, stubby grass. But the savannas close to the rain forests have coarse "elephant grass," which can grow tall enough to hide a person, or even a large animal.

Much of Africa lies in the tropics, but highland regions throughout the continent have a cool and comfortable climate. The Atlas Mountains in the northwest are Africa's longest range. The smaller Drakensberg mountain chain lies along the southeastern tip. Mount Kilimanjaro and Mount Kenya are in the east-central highlands.

These mountains are close to the equator, but they are capped with snow all year. Also in the eastern ranges are Africa's largest lakes, including Lake Tanganyika, the longest fresh-water lake in the world. The waters of the eastern lakes help feed

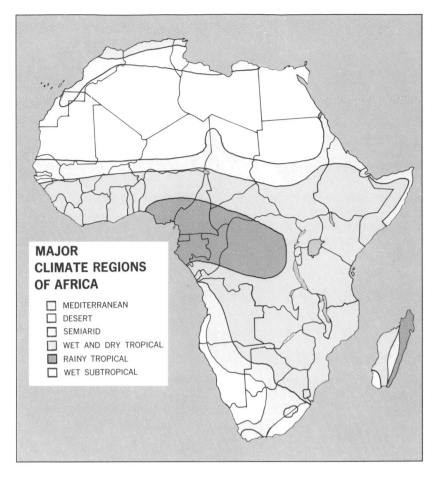

MAJOR CLIMATE REGIONS OF AFRICA

- ☐ MEDITERRANEAN
- ☐ DESERT
- ☐ SEMIARID
- ☐ WET AND DRY TROPICAL
- ▨ RAINY TROPICAL
- ☐ WET SUBTROPICAL

▼ *Africa is a continent rich in wildlife and natural splendors.*

AFRICAN NATIONS

Country	Year of Independence	Area in sq. miles	Area in sq. kilometers	Population	Capital
Algeria	1962	919,662	2,381,741	22,200,000	Algiers
Angola	1975	481,388	1,246,700	900,000	Luanda
Benin	1960	43,487	112,622	4,000,000	Porto Novo
Botswana	1966	231,822	600,372	1,100,000	Gaborone
Burkina Faso	1960	105,877	274,200	6,900,000	Ouagadougou
Burundi	1962	10,747	27,834	4,600,000	Bujumbura
Cameroon	1960	183,582	475,442	9,700,000	Yaoundé
Cape Verde	1975	1,557	4,033	300,000	Praia
Central African Republic	1960	240,553	622,984	2,700,000	Bangui
Chad	1960	495,791	1,284,000	5,200,000	N'Djamena
Comoros	1975	838	2,171	500,000	Moroni
Congo	1960	132,057	342,000	1,700,000	Brazzaville
Djibouti	1977	8,495	22,000	300,000	Djibouti
Egypt	1922	386,690	1,001,449	48,300,000	Cairo
Equatorial Guinea	1968	10,831	28,051	300,000	Malabo
Ethiopia	c. 1000 B.C.	471,812	1,221,900	36,000,000	Addis Ababa
Gabon	1960	103,354	267,667	1,000,000	Libreville
Gambia	1970	4,361	11,295	800,000	Banjul
Ghana	1957	92,106	238,537	14,300,000	Accra
Guinea	1958	94,971	245,957	6,100,000	Conakry
Guinea-Bissau	1974	13,949	36,125	900,000	Bissau
Ivory Coast	1960	124,513	322,463	10,100,000	Abidjan
Kenya	1963	224,977	582,646	20,200,000	Nairobi
Lesotho	1951	11,721	30,355	1,500,000	Maseru
Liberia	1847	43,003	111,369	2,200,000	Monrovia
Libya	1951	679,411	1,759,540	4,000,000	Tripoli
Madagascar	1960	226,674	587,041	10,000,000	Antananarivo
Malawi	1964	45,750	118,484	7,100,000	Lilongwe
Mali	1960	478,801	1,240,000	7,700,000	Bamako
Mauritania	1960	397,984	1,030,700	1,900,000	Nouakchott
Mauritius	1968	805	2,085	1,000,000	Port Louis
Morocco	1956	172,426	446,550	24,300,000	Rabat
Mozambique	1975	302,351	783,030	13,900,000	Maputo
Namibia	IN DISPUTE-CONTROLLED BY SOUTH AFRICA	318,284	824,292	1,100,000	Windhoek
Niger	1960	489,227	1,267,000	6,500,000	Niamey
Nigeria	1960	356,695	923,768	91,200,000	Lagos
Réunion	FRENCH OVERSEAS DEPARTMENT	969	2,510	503,000	St. Denis
Rwanda	1962	10,170	26,338	6,300,000	Kigali
São Tomé and Príncipe	1975	373	965	100,000	São Tomé
Senegal	1960	75,756	196,192	6,700,000	Dakar
Seychelles	1976	108	280	100,000	Victoria
Sierra Leone	1961	27,701	71,740	3,600,000	Freetown
Somali Republic	1960	246,219	637,657	6,500,000	Mogadishu
South Africa	1931	471,479	1,221,037	32,500,000	Cape Town, Pretoria
Sudan	1956	967,570	2,505,813	21,800,000	Khartoum
Swaziland	1968	6,704	17,363	600,000	Mbabane
Tanzania	1964 (UNITED)	364,927	945,087	21,700,000	Dodoma
Togo	1960	21,623	56,000	3,000,000	Lomé
Tunisia	1956	63,175	163,610	7,200,000	Tunis
Uganda	1962	91,141	236,036	14,700,000	Kampala
Western Sahara	IN DISPUTE-OCCUPIED BY MOROCCO	102,703	265,980	95,000	El Aaiún
Zaire	1960	905,633	2,345,709	33,100,000	Kinshasa
Zambia	1964	290,607	752,614	6,800,000	Lusaka
Zimbabwe	1980	150,815	390,580	8,600,000	Harare

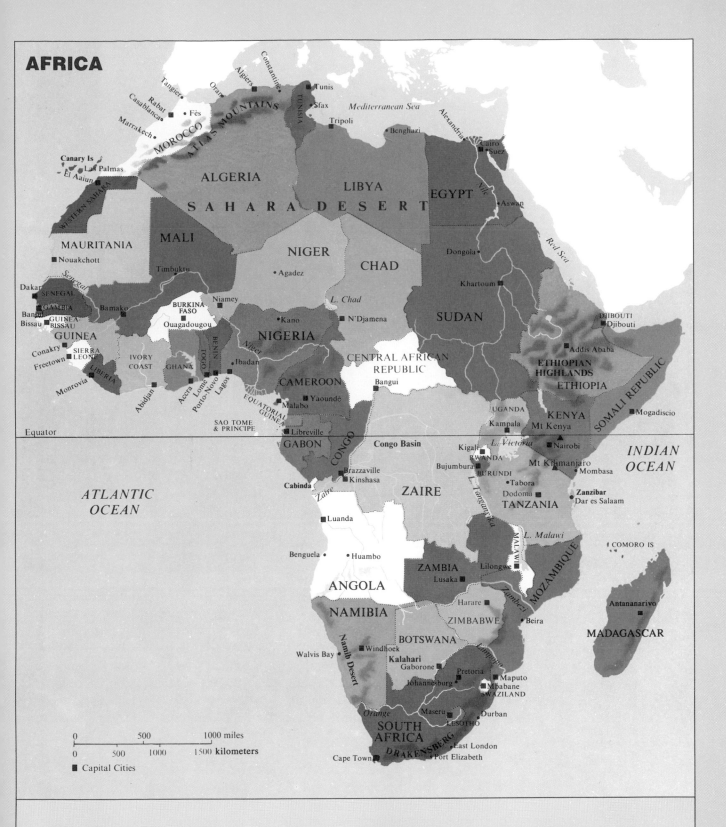

AFRICA

Total Population: 551,000,000.

Total Area: 11,700,000 square miles (30,300,000 sq. km).

Highest Point: Mount Kilimanjaro in Tanzania; 19,565 feet (5,963 m).

Mountain Ranges: Atlas, Drakensberg, Ruwenzori.

Lowest Point: Qattara Depression in northern Egypt; 440 feet (134 m) below sea level.

Longest River: Nile River; 4,160 miles (6,695 km).

Other Major Rivers: Zaire (Congo), Niger, Zambezi.

Largest Lake: Lake Victoria; 26,828 square miles (69,479 sq. km).

Largest City: Cairo (5,881,000 people).

Natural Wonders: Great Rift Valley, Victoria Falls, Sahara Desert (world's largest desert), Lake Tanganyika (world's longest lake).

▶ *Zebras, antelopes, and guinea fowl quench their thirst at a waterhole on the African savanna. In the distance are more antelopes and a lone giraffe.*

▼ *A finely carved ivory mask from West Africa.*

▼ *A Bushman hunter. Bushmen can find food, even in the most barren country and can survive where others would die of hunger and thirst.*

three great rivers—the Nile, the Zaire (Congo), and the Zambezi. Another important river, the Niger, drains the waters of west-central Africa. Steep waterfalls and rapids often occur at the places where these mighty rivers plunge from the high plateaus to the low coastal lands. The spectacular Victoria Falls, on the Zambezi River in southeastern Africa, drop about 335 feet (102 m).

Animal Life Some of the world's most famous animals come from Africa. Giraffes, elephants, zebras, antelopes, and rhinoceroses feed on the plentiful grasses and shrubs of the savannas. Fierce meat-eaters such as lions, leopards, and cheetahs also dwell in the grassy plains. Ostriches, the largest of all birds, are found in the sandy savanna lands near the Sahara. Many of these large animals are protected in special parks, because so many have been killed by hunters.

Crocodiles and hippopotamuses are common in warm rivers and swamps. The tropical rain forests are the home of gorillas, chimpanzees, monkeys, colorful birds, and a great variety of insects and snakes. The rock python

is a giant African snake that squeezes its prey to death and swallows it whole. An especially dreaded insect of the tropical lands is the blood-sucking tsetse fly. It carries the germs that cause sleeping sickness and other diseases.

People Africa has an enormous variety of people, with different customs and ways of life. Most Africans are farmers who live in villages in the grasslands and coastal areas. Many are nomads, who wander from place to place, herding cattle, sheep, or other livestock. Some live and work in modern cities. A few primitive tribes hunt and gather wild plant food. They live much as their ancestors lived for thousands of years.

Negroes (blacks) are the largest group of Africans. They live mainly in regions south of the Sahara Desert. The people of the various African tribes can be quite different in appearance. Many tribes take their names from the languages they speak. The *Bushmen*, a tribe of hunters of the Kalahari Desert, and the *Hottentots*, nomadic herding peoples of the southwest, are sometimes referred to as Negroid (Negro-like). Their yellowish-brown skin makes them different from most other blacks. The *Nilotes* include several tribes, such as the Dinkas, who live in the Nile River Basin. They are rather dark-skinned and are unusually tall and slender. The *Pygmies*, also called Negrillos, rarely grow taller than 4½ feet (1.4 m). They are hunters who live in the tropical rain forests.

North Africans are chiefly Caucasian (white) peoples. Most of them are Arabs and Berbers who dwell north of the Sahara. A few nomadic tribes, such as the *Bedouins*, roam this vast desert, living in tents and tending herds of camels, goats, and sheep. There are more than five million Africans of British, Dutch, French, Spanish, and Portuguese descent. Most of them live in South Africa, with small numbers in Zimbabwe, Kenya, or along the Mediterranean coast, where the climate is much like that of Europe. About a million Asians, mainly of Indian origin, live in eastern and southeastern Africa.

LANGUAGES. Africans speak more than 800 languages. Arabic is the chief tongue of northern Africa. Great numbers of eastern Africans speak Swahili. It is just one of 80 Bantu languages. Hausa is also widely spoken, especially in the west. The Bushmen and Hottentots speak a variety of Khoisan languages, which are quite unusual. They feature clicking sounds that are not found in any other language. English or French are widely spoken in many countries that were once European colonies. The Dutch of South Africa speak Afrikaans, a Germanic language developed by Dutch settlers in the 1600's.

RELIGION. The religions of Africa are as varied as the people. Many different groups have their own tribal religions. Most tribes believe in one god who created the universe and who controls human life. They may also worship their ancestors as minor gods, and believe in spirits that rep-

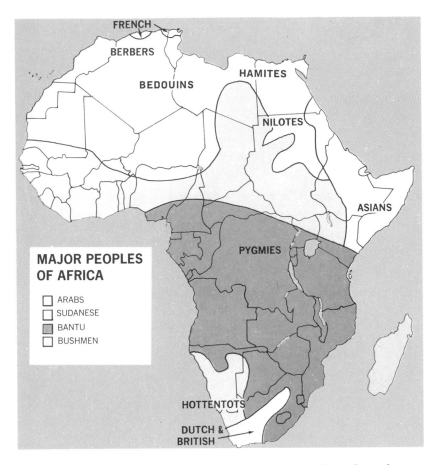

▲ The modern map of Africa overlies the ancient pattern of peoples and cultures. The borders of the modern states of Africa were largely fixed by the European colonial powers. The Bantu are the most widespread African people.

▲ Fishermen in Chad, in central Africa, get their nets ready to go fishing on Lake Chad.

▲ (Left picture) *A modern African woman.* (Right picture) *Traditional business is unchanged in an African market. Here traders still sell grain much as their ancestors did centuries ago.*

▼ *A Zulu woman in a colorful headdress. The Zulus are the largest single group of black African people in South Africa. They number over 4 million.*

resent parts of nature, such as trees, water, or the sun. Religious rituals are an important part of tribal life. They mark events such as births, marriages, and deaths. Magic ceremonies are often performed to heal the sick and to make the land more fertile.

About 145 million Africans, mainly in the north, are Muslims. Many African peoples were converted to Christianity by European missionaries in the 1800's. Large numbers of Egyptians and Ethiopians are members of the Coptic Orthodox Church. About 177,000 people, including several Negro groups, are Jewish.

History Africa has a long and complex history. Fossil bones and other ancient remains found by archeologists show that the human race had its beginnings on the African continent millions of years ago. Rock paintings and tools of the Stone Age have also been discovered. But not much is known about the earliest peoples of Africa. The first highly developed civilization began in Egypt in the Nile Valley about 3,000 B.C. An important area of settlement after 1,000 B.C. was the Mediterranean coast of Africa. Phoenician and Greek invaders founded colonies there. As Egypt gradually became weaker, it was conquered about 725 B.C. by the Kushites, a black society on the Nile

River south of Egypt. The Kushites built the oldest and greatest civilization of black Africa. It lasted a thousand years. Both Egypt and the Mediterranean lands had become part of the Roman Empire by the middle of the first century A.D.

Still another group of invaders, the Muslims of Arabia, began to conquer northern Africa about the year 700. Muslim influence spread in time to west-central Africa, where there were several large black kingdoms. Camel caravans were sent across the Sahara to trade with kingdoms of Ghana, Mali, and Songhai. Northern African goods such as cloth and wheat were exchanged for gold and ivory. Arab traders brought their religion and culture to the coast of eastern Africa, and also captured black slaves.

The next great influence on African development came from Europe. The Portuguese set up trading posts on both the east and west coasts during the 1400's. At first they were interested only in African gold, ivory, and spices. But as colonies began to be established in the Americas, the Portuguese found that the slave trade was even more profitable. The British and French also set up coastal trading posts in the 1600's, and the Dutch started a colony at the Cape of Good Hope. The slave trade began to decline in the 1800's. But millions of black Africans had been captured and brought to the Americas by that time.

European explorers and missionaries penetrated the interior of Africa in the 1770's. Europeans became interested in colonizing Africa when this continent's vast natural resources were discovered. Great Britain, France, Germany, Belgium, Spain, Portugal, and Italy competed for control of Africa, beginning in about 1850. These nations had divided up almost all of Africa among themselves by 1914. Only Ethiopia and Liberia were independent countries.

Colonial rule brought great changes to Africa. Transportation was improved, industries were developed, and new cities were built. Missionaries set up schools and hospitals in remote places. But not all the changes brought about by the Europeans were good. Often the white settlers did not understand the Africans' ways, and they tried to do away with the cherished customs of tribal peoples. Many blacks were offered jobs in mines and factories, but they were not given the same rights and wages as white people. Europeans often took the best lands for themselves, leaving the less productive lands to the Africans. Even the borders of the colonial states were drawn without much regard for the identities and traditional boundaries of the Africans.

People in some parts of Africa began to demand the right of self-government in the late 1880's. The struggle for independence became stronger and more widespread after World War II. A new generation of black African leaders emerged, ready to lead new nations to independence. Most of the colonies gained their independence peacefully during the 1950's and 1960's. Many former French and British colonies kept trading and other links with France and Britain. Portugal was reluctant to give up its African possessions, and only wars in the 1970's finally led to their independence. By the 1980's only the

French-held island of Réunion remained dependent. In South Africa, the whites retained control of the government, but faced growing demands for change from the black majority.

Africa's new nations face many problems. Some enjoy rich natural resources, such as oil and other minerals. But many are poor. Drought, hunger, and civil war have brought hardship to millions of Africans. Ancient ways of life have altered dramatically, with the growth of cities and new industries.

However, enormous advances are being made. Education is now widespread, and each year more Africans are being trained as scientists, engineers, doctors, and business people. Women are playing a leading part in this educational revolution. Art, especially music and literature, is flourishing. In international affairs, including sports, Africa is emerging as a powerful force.

One problem is the difficulty of unifying groups of people with very different traditions and customs. The Organization of African Unity (OAU), established in 1963, promotes economic and political cooperation among African nations and tries to settle disputes peacefully.

For further information on:
Animals, *see* ANIMAL DISTRIBUTION,

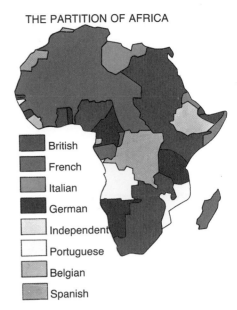

THE PARTITION OF AFRICA

- British
- French
- Italian
- German
- Independent
- Portuguese
- Belgian
- Spanish

▲ *A map showing how Africa was divided, or partitioned, between European states in the late 1800's.*

▼ *Modern buildings line the streets of Nairobi, the capital of Kenya, in east Africa.*

▲ *Louis Agassiz, Swiss-American naturalist, added greatly to our knowledge of fish and geology.*

NATIONAL PARK, RARE ANIMAL.

Arts, *see* ART HISTORY, FOLK ART, MUSICAL INSTRUMENTS.

History, *see* ANCIENT CIVILIZATIONS; BOER WAR; CARTHAGE; DIAS, BARTHOLOMEU; EGYPT, ANCIENT; GAMA, VASCO DA; LIVINGSTONE, DAVID; RHODES, CECIL; SCHWEITZER, ALBERT; SLAVERY; SONGHAI EMPIRE; STANLEY, HENRY MORTON; WORLD WAR II.

Language, *see* ALPHABET, ARABIC, LANGUAGES.

People, *see* CIVILIZATION, HUMAN BEINGS, PYGMY.

Physical Features, *see* CONTINENT, EQUATOR, JUNGLE, MEDITERRANEAN SEA, NILE RIVER, RED SEA, SAHARA DESERT, ZAIRE RIVER.

Also read the article on each country shown in the table.

People, on average, live much longer in developed countries than in the underdeveloped world. In Sweden, for example, 22 percent of the population is over 65. In Zimbabwe, only 3 percent of people reach that age. Half the population of Zimbabwe is under 15.

AGASSIZ, LOUIS (1807–1873)

The ambitious son of a villager in Switzerland grew up to be one of the greatest naturalists of the 1800's. He was Jean Louis Agassiz. He gained his greatest fame for important work in *ichthyology*, the study of fish. He was a geologist who added to scientific understanding of glaciers and the ways continents form.

Even as a child in Switzerland, Agassiz was determined to be a great naturalist. He formed the habit of observing nature closely. This habit became the key to his life's work. He had to see nature at first hand, not just read about it in books. Once he risked his life to go into the center of a glacier to study it. Agassiz was a teacher as well as a scientist. He had a warm personality and was popular.

When he came to America at the age of 39, Agassiz was already world famous. He became a professor at Harvard University, and he founded Harvard's Museum of Comparative Zoology.

ALSO READ: GEOLOGY, ZOOLOGY.

AGING On each birthday a person adds one year to his age. Growing older year by year is called *chronological* aging.

However, each person grows and ages at his own pace. Some babies take longer than others to learn to walk. Some children grow faster than others. Scientists believe that each person has a "biological clock" that sets his speed of aging. Most plants keep growing throughout their lives, but most animals do not. A human being is usually full grown by age 21.

Scientists divide human life into three periods—youth, middle age, and old age. In youth, the speed with which the body obeys orders from the mind, called *coordination*, is quickest. The muscles of young people move easily and usually do not stay stiff or tired for long after hard work or play. People's muscles tire more quickly in middle age.

As it ages, some parts of the body weaken, while others remain strong. Parts of the body wear out at different speeds. Some worn-out parts of the body can be replaced. For example, heart valves (that pump blood) can be replaced by artificial valves that work as well as natural ones. Hip joints can also be replaced by artificial bones.

Many older people with frail bodies may still have very active minds. The growth of the mind may be at a different rate from the aging of the rest of the body.

ALSO READ: ANIMAL, GROWTH, HUMAN BODY, PLANT.

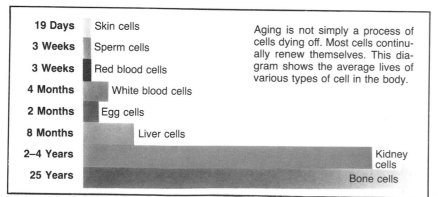

19 Days	Skin cells
3 Weeks	Sperm cells
3 Weeks	Red blood cells
4 Months	White blood cells
2 Months	Egg cells
8 Months	Liver cells
2–4 Years	Kidney cells
25 Years	Bone cells

Aging is not simply a process of cells dying off. Most cells continually renew themselves. This diagram shows the average lives of various types of cell in the body.

AGRICULTURE Life for human beings was difficult before they found out how to grow food. Prehistoric people lived in small groups, because it was difficult for a large number of people to find food. The groups roamed the countryside, constantly looking for animals to kill or wild plants to pick. If they could not spear or trap an animal, and if they did not find plants, they went hungry. Agriculture, often called the "mother of civilization," changed all that.

The word *agriculture* comes from two Latin words meaning "to plant and to care for the fields." But agriculture is far more than planting and raising crops. Agricultural scientists today study soil, climate, how plants grow, how to stop plant disease, and how to develop better plants. They also study farm animals. They try to find new ways to raise better animals, and to prevent and cure diseases. Farms, ranches, plantations, orchards, gardens, dairies, sheds for beehives, and a great many laboratories and factories are now parts of agriculture. The areas where most plants and animals are cared for are called *rural areas*. "Rural" is an adjective meaning "open country."

Agriculture employs more than half the people on Earth. But in the United States, only about 3 out of every 100 working people work full or part-time on farms. Many machines are used on North American farms, ranches, and plantations. Scientific methods are used in crop production and livestock care. Although they are a small group of people, U.S. farmers produce more food each year than all the people in the United States can eat.

Other parts of the world cannot run farms with so few people as the U.S. does. Three of the main reasons for this are the lack of good cropland, the cost of buying and using machines, and the slow change away from ancient ways of farming. About 60 out of every 100 people in Africa live in rural areas and work on the land. About 15 out of every 100 people in Europe are "farm folk." So are about 55 out of every 100 in Asia, and 40 out of every 100 in South America. Some of the cattle and sheep stations (ranches) in Australia cover thousands of square miles, and about 20 out of every 100 Australians live and work in farm areas.

The Start of Agriculture People living in the sunny, fertile lands between the Mediterranean Sea and the Persian Gulf are believed to have started agriculture more than 10,000 years ago. The first farmers discovered that wild seeds planted in plots, kept clean of weeds, and watered regularly produced reliable harvests. They lived near their plots to guard them from both human and animal robbers. So, instead of wandering, they settled down to live in huts by their fields, with nearby pits for storing crops. After a time these places became villages. Then roads were made between the villages, and peoples became acquainted.

The first animal to live side by side with people was probably the dog, which was used in hunting. Animals such as goats, sheep, and pigs were hunted, not kept on farms. The first farm animal to be tamed, or *domesticated*, was probably the goat. Soon sheep too were domesticated, then— hundreds of years apart—chickens,

▲ *A wall picture of ancient Egypt shows the time when all work in agriculture was done by hand, using animals and simple tools.*

In ancient Egypt farmers sowed seed in the fertile mud left after the Nile River's yearly flood. Today, canals drain the floodwater into basins. After about eight weeks, the basins are emptied and farmers plant crops in the rich silt the Nile water leaves behind.

cently, slow transportation forced dairy and poultry farmers to keep their animals close to the cities. Today, in Asia and Africa there are still peoples called *nomads* (wanderers) who live as herders. They move from place to place, seeking food and water for their herds.

ONE-CROP FARMING. The ancient Greeks discovered many uses for the fruit and wood of the olive tree. Some Greeks became specialists in growing olives and processing olive oil. Many Egyptian farmers specialized in growing and harvesting cotton. They learned how to harvest the puffy bolls of the cotton plant, remove the seeds, and weave the fibers into cloth. The efforts of the ancient Greeks and the Egyptians were the beginnings of another major branch of agriculture—one-crop farming.

Examples of one-crop agriculture in the U.S. today are the Midwest wheat farms, the southern cotton plantations, and the citrus groves of Florida and California. Each of these places, as well as many other farming areas in the world, has climate and soil that are very good for the one crop of the region.

DIVERSIFIED FARMING. Several different crops can be grown on one farm. *Diversified farming* was, and still

▲ *In early times, villages were formed where people joined together to care for the fields. Work was done with simple tools. (Top picture.) The scythe was used for mowing for many centuries. (Middle picture.) The harvester machine was invented in 1830. It picked up cut wheat automatically, while workers tied the bundles of grain by hand. (Lower picture.)*

pigs, cattle, donkeys, and finally horses. Domestication of these animals took place mostly along the shores of the Mediterranean, and farther east, on the grassy plains of Russia, called *steppes*, between the Black Sea and the Caspian Sea. These changes caused agriculture to split into three major divisions.

Kinds of Agriculture STOCK FARM-ING. Some families chose to tame and care for herds of animals. These were the herders. In the years of the American Wild West, herders, especially cattle ranchers and shepherds, often lived on the frontier. Until re-

▲ *Small American farms are fast disappearing. They are being combined into large farms where big and powerful machinery can be used more easily, and crops and livestock tended more economically.*

AGRICULTURAL MARKETING IN THE UNITED STATES

If certain products were added up and divided among the 225 million people in the United States, here's an idea of how much each person would get.

	17 chickens for each person	**Total** 3,900,000,000
	1/2 of a turkey for each person	140,000,000
	1/4 of a hog for each person	60,000,000
	1/2 of a cow or steer for each person	116,000,000
	1/20 of a sheep for each person	12,000,000

▲ *Women picking olives, which have ripened and fallen from the trees. Olives are an important crop in the warmer lands of Europe.*

THE COMBINE HARVESTER

1. Rotating blades
2. Cutting bar
3. Auger lifts stems.
4. Conveyer
5. Thresher
6. Sieve separates grain from stalks.
7. Fan
8. Conveyer for grain
9. Conveyer for straw
10. Storage tank for grain
11. Bale binder

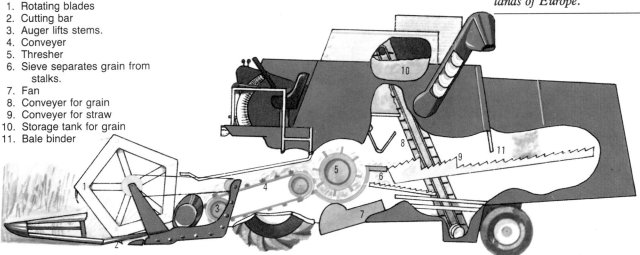

is, the most common type of farming. It got its start in America from European farmers such as those from Estremadura, in Spain. They brought their knowledge of this farming to the New World.

European Farming in America
Spanish soldiers conquered Mexico and Peru and first explored the southern and southwestern U.S. between 1521 and 1550. These Spaniards were called *conquistadors*, meaning "conquerors." Many of them grew up in Estremadura, one of the most beautiful areas of diversified farming in Europe. It is a region of many mountains, river valleys, and red-earth fields along the border between Spain and Portugal. It has been famous for more than 2,000 years for its crops of wheat, olives, fruit, and cork, and for its herds of sheep, goats, and pigs.

The conquistadors quickly realized that the mountains, plains, and climate of Southern California, Arizona, and New Mexico were very much like the countryside and weather of their Spanish homeland. The first Spanish settlers in the Southwest planted the crops they had known in Estremadura—oranges, olives, figs, grapes, and wheat. They brought cattle, horses, and pigs from Spain, too.

▶ *Combine harvesters in an Australian wheatfield. With machines, today's farmers can produce bigger crops with less labor.*

▲ *In parts of the world ancient farm methods are still used. Here an Asian farmer plows a flooded rice field with the help of oxen.*

Machinery has completely changed the farmer's life. Before 1830, cutting an acre of wheat by hand took about 40 hours. Now a large combine-harvester can cut and thresh an acre of wheat in seven minutes.

Spanish settlers also moved into Florida, in the last half of the sixteenth century. The climate and soil of their new home reminded them of Andalusia, the region of Spain that is Estremadura's southern neighbor. So these settlers brought oranges from Andalusia and found that this fruit grew well in Florida. They learned about a New World plant food when they received the small, sweet nuts of the pine-nut tree from Indians. The Indians had used these *piniones* in soups, breads, and candies for a long time.

The French founded New Orleans and began other settlements along the Gulf of Mexico. They, like the Spanish, thought of their European homes when they began to farm. They brought pears and carrots from France to America.

Colonists in Massachusetts and Virginia found their land and climate much like that of their native England. So they brought familiar animals, such as sheep and cattle, and plants, such as apples, to America. These settlers also got help from the Indians, who taught them how to plant and raise corn, squash, and tobacco.

All these New World settlers were fortunate that their new homes were much like their old ones. Plants from

one part of the world cannot easily be grown in other parts. Plants do well in certain soils and climates. In different soils, or in different weather conditions, they may not grow at all.

Names for Agricultural Land The three most common names for agricultural property come from the regions where European methods of caring for the land began. The words *ranch*, *plantation*, and *farm* are really lessons in the history of both language and agriculture.

Ranch comes from the Spanish word *rancho*, which first meant "where the cattle graze." It was used by the Spanish people who pioneered the Rio Grande Valley of New Mexico in 1598. The word spread to Texas, Arizona, and California, and then moved eastward. Most ranches today are west of the Mississippi River, but many of them have no cattle at all. They include mink ranches, horse ranches, fruit ranches, and even rose ranches.

Plantation comes from a Latin word used in the Middle Ages in England to mean a rural estate where servants tended the crops and cared for livestock. Virginians began to develop large one-crop areas of tobacco or rice. Agricultural properties throughout the South were often called plantations, especially where planters owned slaves to do the hard work. Dairy herds, beef cattle, poultry, fruit, grains, beans, vegetables, and peanuts have now become important agricultural products in the South. Diversified farming has replaced much one-crop farming. Agriculturists in the South now prefer to be called farmers instead of planters.

Farm is an old English word that the Pilgrims brought to New England. The word originally meant "land that is rented." The man who worked a farm was not a serf or peasant, but paid an annual rent to the lord or knight who owned the land. If an agriculturist owned his own land, but was not a knight or lord, he was called a *franklin*.

Technology Comes to Agriculture

Abraham Lincoln was President in 1863. At that time, seven out of every ten Americans worked and lived on farms, plantations, and ranches. Nearly everybody owned a horse, and almost every home had a horsebarn and a horse pasture. Horse-power was the chief method of getting the job done. Horses plowed and tilled the fields, hauled the wagons, carriages, coaches, and harvesting machines, and trampled the kernels of grain free from the stalks on the threshing floors. Horses and mules were the great servants of American agriculture from 1600 until 1920. Slaves on Southern plantations also played a very important part in shaping modern American farming.

Tractors, trucks, and hundreds of planting, spraying, weeding, and harvesting machines took the place of horses and mules in the 1920's. Scientists discovered ways to grow two or three times as much crop on the same amount of land. These inventions and discoveries made it possible for a family to farm three, four, or five times as much land as they could have with horses and mules. Fewer people were needed on farms. Machines and other materials needed for modern agriculture were expensive and complicated. Large properties and scientific training became necessary for successful farming. More and more farmers and ranches sold their lands and moved to town. Hired workers were laid off or went to cities for better jobs. In 1900 about 35 of every 100 people in the U.S. worked on farms. Today, only 3 of every 100 people are employed in agriculture.

A major division of the U.S. Government is the Department of Agriculture. Its director, the Secretary of Agriculture, is a member of the President's Cabinet. Working for the Department are thousands of scientists, engineers, economists, and other specialists in modern agriculture. Each state in the U.S. has its own department of agriculture. Many also have a state college of agriculture. The local advisers on agricultural affairs in each area, who have offices at each of the 3,000 county seats in the U.S., are called *county agents*.

Agriculture still faces big problems despite the great changes brought

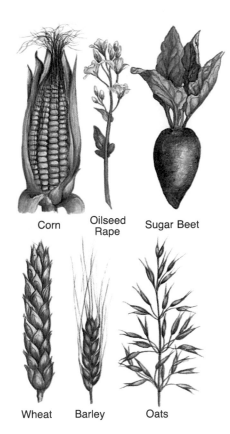

Corn   Oilseed   Sugar Beet
        Rape

Wheat   Barley   Oats

▲ *Farmers produce many crops. But certain plants are favored, because they provide basic foods. Here are six common farm crops.*

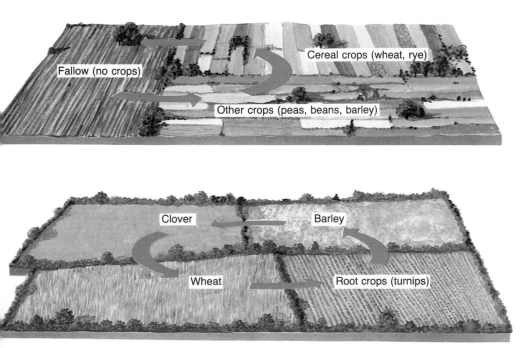

Fallow (no crops)

Cereal crops (wheat, rye)

Other crops (peas, beans, barley)

Clover   Barley

Wheat   Root crops (turnips)

◀ *Farmers know it is unwise to plant the same crops in the same fields year after year. This exhausts the soil and helps the buildup of plant diseases, so that poor yields result. Instead, farmers plan to grow crops in rotation, so that no field is seeded with the same crops two years running. Here are shown two examples: a three-year rotation, where the land is allowed to rest, or lie fallow, one year (top picture); and a four-year rotation (bottom picture), where a new crop is grown in each field every year.*

▲ *A traditional farmland scene, with small fields and grazing dairy cattle. Such farms are common in parts of Europe as well as America.*

People have bred sheep, hogs, cattle, and poultry for thousands of years. Chickens now lay at least 250 eggs per year, which is 15 times more than wild hens lay. Cows now produce more than 1,000 gallons (4,000 l) of milk each year, which is about 20 times more than a wild cow produces.

about by machines and science. In the developed world, such as the United States and Europe, farmers can produce far more food than is needed by their own people. This extra food creates a *surplus*, which may be thrown away. Yet in other parts of the world, such as in the desert lands of Africa, millions of people are hungry. Here local agriculture is suffering from climatic change, and from a breakdown of old village ways as people leave the land and move to the new towns.

By using sensible "intermediate" technology (some machines and fertilizers, but not so much that small farmers are driven out of business), countries like India have done much to feed their hungry people. Agricultural experts are working to find better ways of feeding everyone.

■ **LEARN BY DOING**

Farmers who want to do well must make important decisions and answer questions before choosing which crops to plant. Is the lawn around your house or in a park nearby thick and green and fun to walk barefoot in all summer? Or does it turn brown and scratchy and ugly? What grass is

best for your lawn? What flowers will grow in your garden? What kinds of fruit and vegetables will do well? These questions are similar to the ones that farmers must answer. Suppose that you are a farmer getting ready to choose the "crops" (plants) for your "farm" (your backyard). You must answer these questions if you want to have a successful farm.

You can get the answers to these questions from the department of agriculture of your state. The scientists who work there have studied these questions very carefully. They have lists of plants for your area. If you send them a small jar of soil from your "farm," they will tell you exactly what kinds of plants will or will not grow well.

Write to the agriculture department, and ask for information on plants that do well in your area. Also get an analysis (test) of your soil. Then, working with the results of the analysis and with the list of "crops," choose what to plant. ■

For further information on:
Conservation, *see* CONSERVATION, FERTILIZER, IRRIGATION, NATURAL RESOURCES, SOIL.
Crops, *see* CORN, FRUIT, RICE, VEGETABLES, WHEAT.
Farm Life, *see* FARM MACHINERY, WEATHER.
Livestock, *see* CATTLE, GOAT, HORSE, POULTRY, SHEEP, VETERINARY MEDICINE.
Processes, *see* DAIRY FARMING, FISHING INDUSTRY, FOOD, MEAT, PLANT BREEDING.

AIDS see VIRUS.

AIR Air is all around you. You cannot see it, smell it, or taste it. But you can feel the wind blow. You can see the wind move waves on the water, clouds in the sky, and tree branches. Wind is moving air.

Without air you could not breathe.

There could be no living plants or animals. Because sound travels through air, without air there would be silence. The movement of invisible air can support a large, heavy airplane. Air makes up a precious blanket of atmosphere wrapped around the Earth. Beyond this blanket lies airless space. Humans must carry their own air supplies to be able to live and work when they travel in spaceships through this airless space.

Air is a mixture of gases and water vapor. The most important gases in the air are nitrogen and oxygen. About 78 percent of the air is made up of nitrogen, and about 21 percent of oxygen. The remaining one percent is mostly argon, plus very tiny amounts of some other gases. Almost all living things use the oxygen in air. Fire cannot burn without oxygen.

When air expands, it becomes lighter. This fact allows a small electric heater to heat an entire room. The heater warms the air next to it. The warmed air becomes lighter and moves upward. Cool air moves into its place. The new air gets warm and also rises. Then it cools and moves down. The air keeps moving in circles, and the whole room is soon heated.

■ LEARN BY DOING

AIR CAN BE COMPRESSED. Get a small paper bag and blow into it until it swells up. Close the bag by twisting the end. Feel the bag. If the bag were just standing open, it would be filled with air. But by blowing into the bag, you have forced even more air into the same amount of space. The air from your lungs has been *compressed*, or squeezed together, in the bag, so the bag feels firm.

Now lay an empty bag on the edge of a table. Place a small book on top of it. Blow the bag full of air. The book will be lifted from the table. It is held up by the air in the bag. In the same way, air in tires holds a car off the ground. You are really riding on compressed air when you ride in a car.

AIR EXPANDS WHEN HEATED. Fasten a balloon containing a little air to the open top of each of two small-necked bottles. Place one bottle in a pan of hot water and the other in ice water. The air in the first bottle is heated by the hot water. The *molecules* (small particles) of air move faster and faster. The air *expands* and moves into the balloon. The balloon gets bigger. Air in the other bottle cools and takes up less space than before, so the balloon shrinks and looks nearly empty.

AIR IS EVERYWHERE. Pack a glass full of soil from a garden. Add water to the glass. Watch the bubbles of air rise through the water. A lawn is often dotted with earthworms after a rain. The rain has forced air out of the ground, so the worms must come to the surface to breathe. ■

ALSO READ: AIRPLANE, AIR PRESSURE, ATMOSPHERE, GAS, WATER CYCLE, WEATHER.

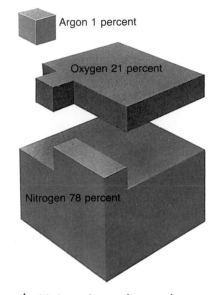

▲ *Air is made up of gases. As this diagram shows, nitrogen is the most common, making up 78 percent of the air.*

Air is heavier than you think. The average roomful of air weighs more than 100 pounds (45 kg).

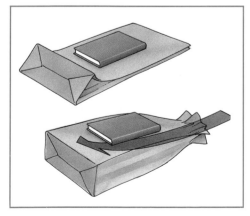

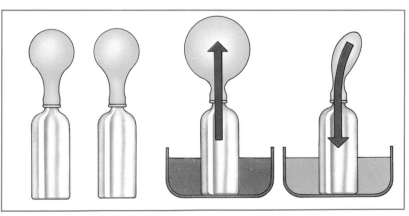

AIR CONDITIONING

AIR CONDITIONING Air is seldom at the temperature comfortable for most people—about 70°F (21°C). So we have learned to build machines that change air temperature. Machines that raise the air temperature are heaters. Machines that lower the air temperature are air conditioners. The work that these machines do is called *air conditioning*.

■ LEARN BY DOING

You can make a simple *air conditioner*. You need an electric fan, a bowl of ice cubes, a thermometer, and an adult to help you. Put the fan on a table, and put the thermometer on the table about 15 inches (38 cm) in front of the fan. Note what temperature the thermometer shows. Now turn on the fan, but be careful. Do not go near the fan while it is running. You can feel a cool breeze when you stand in front of the fan. Wait five minutes and see what temperature the thermometer then shows. Next, place the bowl of ice on the table, just in front of the fan. Is the breeze even cooler? After five minutes, what temperature does the thermometer show? ■

Air conditioners have other jobs besides changing the air temperature. The amount of water vapor in the air is called *humidity*. Humidity is also important to comfort. A person's per-spiration usually evaporates into the air. This makes the person feel cool. (Put a drop of rubbing alcohol on your arm and blow on it. What happens?) But in summer, the humidity is often high. The air has no room for evaporated perspiration. So air conditioners remove water from the air. Perspiration evaporates and a person feels cool.

One more important job for air conditioners is to filter, or clean, the air. Air is filled with dust, pollen, and many other substances. Air conditioner filters are made of fine threads of glass called *glass wool*. The air conditioner's fan blows the air through the filter, which catches the dust.

Many home air conditioners are small, and fit in windows. Larger buildings often have *central* air conditioning, and one big machine cools the entire building. Pipes carry cool air from the machine to all the rooms. And sometimes the same pipes that carry cool air in summer carry hot air in winter. Many modern automobiles too have a controlled air conditioning system. So do passenger airplanes, railroad cars, ships, and television studios (where there are very hot lights).

ALSO READ: GAS, HEATING, HUMIDITY, REFRIGERATION.

AIRCRAFT CARRIER An aircraft carrier is a huge ship with a military airport on its top deck. On board are workshops that repair airplanes; places to store ammunition, bombs, and fuel; and almost everything else that would be found at a military airport. Thousands of people live and work on board this floating town.

Most jet airplanes need a long runway on which to gain the speed needed to take off or to lose speed on landing. Airports on land usually have runways about 10,000 feet

▼ *A window air conditioner takes warm air from the outside and sends cool, clean air into a house. The blower sucks in warm air. The filter cleans out dust and dirt. The evaporator has cold coils, which cool the air and remove moisture from it. The condenser fan blows air over the condenser to make the gas in the coils turn to a cooling liquid. The compressor is a motor that squeezes and pumps the gas through the coils. The blower does its second task by blowing cool air into the room.*

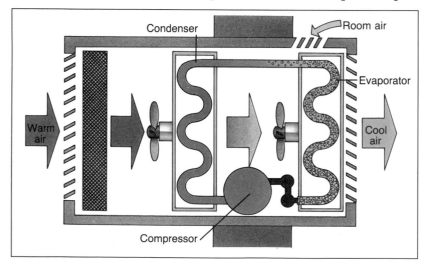

Condenser

Room air

Evaporator

Warm air

Cool air

Compressor

(3,000 m) long. Because there is not this much room on a carrier, planes are "thrown" into the air moving fast enough to fly. A carrier plane is launched much as a small model glider is catapulted into the air with a rubber band. Hooks on the airplane are attached to a powerful steam catapult or "slingshot" that runs down a track on the deck.

On landing, another hook on the tail of an airplane catches cables strung across the flight deck. The ends of the cables are attached to cylinders that move in a big pipe filled with oil. The cables relax or "give" when an airplane first catches them, but they bring it to a stop in about 125 feet (38 m). Some planes, such as vertical take-off "jump jets" and helicopters, can take off from and land on a carrier without these aids.

History Aircraft carriers got their start on November 14, 1910. On that day Eugene Ely flew an airplane off a wooden platform on the cruiser USS *Birmingham.* Aircraft carriers were not important in World War I, because they were not practical. But in 1918 the British navy built the first true aircraft carrier, called HMS

▼ *The U.S. Navy nuclear-powered carrier* Nimitz. *Built in 1971, this mighty ship can carry 90 airplanes and helicopters.*

Argus. The first U.S. carrier was the USS *Langley* (1922).

Aircraft carriers became really important when Japan bombed Pearl Harbor, Hawaii, on December 7, 1941. The airplanes that carried the bombs came from Japanese aircraft carriers. This surprise attack came near to crippling the United States Navy stationed in the Pacific.

During three great naval battles (Midway, Coral Sea and Leyte Gulf) fought between June and October,

▲ *Looking down on the flight decks of the U.S.S.* Enterprise. *The carrier has two flight decks, and can launch four jets at a time, as seen here. Other jets are moving into position for take-off. A carrier task force can quickly display its formidable power in any trouble spot around the world.*

▲ *The USS* Langley, *a converted coal-carrying ship, was the Navy's first aircraft carrier. It went into service in 1922, carrying biplanes (two-winged airplanes).*

▲ *Cables across the flight deck slow down a landing plane. A hook underneath the plane catches the cable.*

1944, planes from U.S. aircraft carriers destroyed almost all of the Japanese carrier fleet. U.S. carriers had assured an Allied victory in the Pacific during World War II.

Carriers Today After the war, aircraft carriers were enlarged and improved. Steam-powered catapults and angled flight decks permitted carriers to launch jet planes. Helicopters also proved effective as carrier-borne aircraft. The Soviet Union began to develop its carrier fleet from the 1960's. Today, the U.S. and the Soviet Union have the most powerful carriers in the world. Other nations, such as France and Britain, have small carriers.

The U.S. Navy has five nuclear-powered attack aircraft carriers: the *Enterprise*, *Nimitz*, *Eisenhower*, *Vinson*, and *Theodore Roosevelt*. The *Nimitz* is the world's largest warship in *displacement tonnage*. It displaces (occupies) 93,400 long tons (94,900 tonnes) of water when fully loaded. The *Nimitz* is 1,092 feet (333 m) long. The deck where the airplanes take off and land is 254 feet (77 m) wide. In combat or on patrol duty, *Nimitz*-class vessels carry about 6,300 crew members and 100 aircraft.

Other U.S. attack carriers are powered by oil. They include the *Kitty Hawk*, *John F. Kennedy*, and *Forrestal*, each of which carries about 4,900 persons and 85 airplanes. Another type of carrier is equipped with

complicated electronic devices to find and destroy enemy submarines. And there are also special carriers which carry marines, their helicopters and landing craft, and the jet planes to support them.

Military experts argue about which is more useful—aircraft carriers or land-based airplanes. Both are expensive. The people who favor carriers claim that carriers can be anywhere in the world in a short time. Land airfields overseas may not always be usable. But the floating airport—the carrier—is ready whenever it is needed. Moreover, aircraft carriers with nuclear power plants can run for as long as 13 years without refueling.

ALSO READ: AIRPORT, NAVY, SUBMARINE, WORLD WAR II.

AIR CUSHION VEHICLE (ACV) An air cushion vehicle, or *hovercraft*, is a machine that rides on a layer of *compressed air* that holds it off the ground or water. It may ride only a few inches or several feet above the surface, depending on the vehicle's design. The advantage of being off the surface is that there is less friction between the machine and the surface. Friction is a force that opposes movement when one object or surface is rubbed against another. It is caused, for example, by a car's wheels turning against the ground, or by a boat's hull moving through water. The more friction there is between a vehicle and the ground or water, the slower the vehicle travels.

You probably cannot push even a small car. You would fight the weight of the car and the friction of its wheels on the axles. But if a strong wind underneath the car lifted it straight up, even one inch, you could probably move the car as long as the air held it off the ground. All you would have to do is push the car through air, and the friction between the car and the air would be very little. The wind would be an *air cushion*. An air cushion can also be formed by a strong wind blowing down from the car, to lift if off the ground. Air cushion vehicles use large fans to create the strong wind.

Air cushion vehicles (ACVs) come in several designs. One works only over water. Another must follow a big track. Other ACVs can travel over any flat surface.

Scientists and inventors thought of these machines as early as 1716. But they did not have the materials or the powerful engines to make them work. The first ACVs that really "flew" were built in the early 1950's. Big fans made the air cushions that lifted the vehicles off the ground. Propellers or jet engine exhausts then drove them forward.

Modern ACVs usually look like boats. Several fans may work to push the air down, and as many as four large propellers push the machine forward. ACVs can travel over land or water at up to 80 miles an hour (130 km/hr). ACVs that follow tracks are faster, up to 150 miles an hour (240 km/hr).

Some ACVs have skirts made of a rubber-like material. These skirts are attached around the bottom of the machine. They hold the air cushion in place. An ACV with skirts can ride as high as 10 feet (3 m) above the surface. It can jump wide ditches and cross marshes. ACVs can travel over ice and snow, and over deserts.

Large hovercraft ferries that carry 175 passengers and 35 automobiles cross the English Channel between England and France. But so far ACVs have not proved as successful as was at first hoped.

ALSO READ: AIR PRESSURE, TRANSPORTATION.

SRN4 Hovercraft

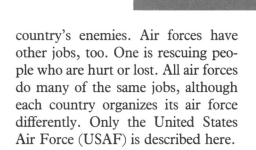

country's enemies. Air forces have other jobs, too. One is rescuing people who are hurt or lost. All air forces do many of the same jobs, although each country organizes its air force differently. Only the United States Air Force (USAF) is described here.

USAF Combat Commands The *Military Airlift Command* (MAC) is one of the four main combat commands of the USAF. MAC furnishes air transportation for the Army, Navy, and Air Force. It carries anything needed in a hurry. MAC has all kinds of aircraft, from small helicopters to the huge C-5A jet transport. The C-5A is almost as long as a football field and can carry tanks and trucks, or as many as 900 soldiers.

MAC also runs a rescue service. It has helicopters and special airplanes to pick up wounded soldiers and air crew shot down over enemy territory. The rescue service has bases in many countries. It has saved many civilians who got lost or had accidents on mountains or in canyons, forests,

▲ *A large ferry hovercraft. This kind of ground-effect craft skims over the water, supported by a cushion of air. The air is held in place by the craft's flexible skirt. Four propellers push the craft along.*

The U.S. Air Force has about 4,000 combat airplanes, but a total of 600,000 people. At the end of World War II (1945), the Air Force had 80,000 airplanes and nearly 2½ million people.

AIR FORCE One job of an air force is to defend its country by using airplanes and missiles against the

▲ *The B-52 Stratofortress is a long-range heavy bomber. It can carry air-to-surface guided missiles as well as bombs. The B-52 was the most commonly used U.S. bomber from the 1950's to the 1970's, and is still in service.*

▲ *An airman trying on a flight suit at an officer training school. Here, trainee officers undergo a course of study and exercise.*

deserts, or snowstorms. At the President's request, MAC flies medicines, doctors, food, and supplies to countries where there have been earthquakes, floods, and other disasters.

A special MAC squadron flies the President of the United States and his staff all over the world. The people in the squadron, from pilots to mechanics to clerks, are carefully picked. The squadron's aircraft range from small helicopters to big jet transports. The squadron is often called the *Air Force One Squadron*, because any airplane the President flies in is *Air Force One*.

The *Strategic Air Command* (SAC) is another major part of the USAF. SAC is set up to attack military bases and factories in an enemy's country in case of war. SAC's main weapons are bombers and guided missiles. The B-52 is the biggest bomber. It can carry atom bombs and cruise missiles. It can fly halfway around the world, at 650 miles an hour (1,050 km/hr), without refueling. Another bomber, smaller and faster, is the F-111. For long-range missions, bombers can be refueled while flying, by a *tanker airplane*. The tanker hooks up with the

bomber in flight and pumps fuel into its tanks.

SAC's intercontinental ballistic missiles (ICBMs) are kept in deep, concrete-lined holes in the ground, called *silos*. An ICBM carries an atom bomb in the nose. It can travel 7,000 miles (11,000 km) at 15,000 miles an hour (24,000 km/hr) and is very difficult to intercept. Atomic missiles can be fired only by direct order from the President of the United States. They have never been fired.

The *Aerospace Defense Command* (ADC) operates from a huge cave drilled out of a mountain, near Colorado Springs, Colorado. It has computers, radar, telephones, and radios to keep in touch with bases around the world. Its job is to protect the U.S. from enemy airplanes and missiles. ADC shares its cave with a group from Canada. Together, they make up the North American Air Defense Command (NORAD).

To shoot down enemy airplanes flying over Canada or the U.S., NORAD would use *fighter-interceptors* and *surface-to-air missiles* (SAMs). Fighter-interceptors are airplanes which can fly fast and high. The F-15 Eagle is a fighter-interceptor that carries *air-to-air guided missiles* (AAMs). Another form of defense is the surface-to-air missile, such as the Patriot, which is fired from the ground like a rocket.

The job of *Tactical Air Command* (TAC) is to help the Army in its ground operations. TAC has fighter-bombers to carry bombs, cannons, rockets, and guided missiles to shoot at enemy tanks, trucks, trains, and storage places for ammunition.

The Air Force also works, usually secretly, to find out what enemy countries are doing. This is called *reconnaissance*. Reconnaissance satellites circle the Earth and take pictures of enemy territory. Reconnaissance planes can fly 2,000 miles an hour (3,200 km/hr) at 80,000 feet (24,000 m)—twice as high as most airliners. Cameras in these planes photograph tiny details. Experts can even recognize different kinds of cars in such pictures!

Other USAF commands train the personnel of the Air Force, handle supplies, and support the combat commands. The USAF at present has about 7,000 combat planes and almost 604,000 people. The people must be highly trained to take care of complicated airplanes, missiles, and radio and radar equipment.

History of the Air Force The U.S. Air Force started August 1, 1907, as part of the Army Signal Corps, with one officer and two enlisted men. The division got its first plane in 1909, from the Wright brothers.

No American airplanes flew in combat during World War I. By the end of that war in 1918, the U.S. had 58,000 Air Service officers and men in France. Many of them had learned to fly in France and Britain.

From earliest days, Army pilots did not want to be controlled by Army ground forces. Most ground generals did not understand the airplane. They thought it should be used as a sort of long-range gun on the battlefield. The pilots believed airplanes should carry the war to an enemy's country and destroy its ability to make war. Military leaders were slow to recognize the importance of the airplane. U.S. General Billy Mitchell, assistant chief of the Air Service, argued for a large independent air force. His public criticism of the War and

AIR FORCE INSIGNIA

United States

Great Britain

Soviet Union

China (People's Republic)

◀ *The F-111 is a swing-wing bomber, which first saw service during the Vietnam War. The picture shows the aircraft's wings open, for slow-speed flight.*

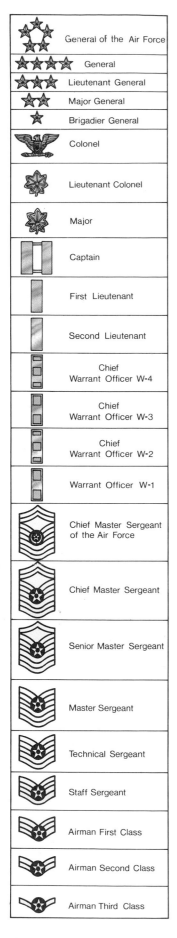

★★★★★	General of the Air Force
★★★★	General
★★★	Lieutenant General
★★	Major General
★	Brigadier General
	Colonel
	Lieutenant Colonel
	Major
	Captain
	First Lieutenant
	Second Lieutenant
	Chief Warrant Officer W-4
	Chief Warrant Officer W-3
	Chief Warrant Officer W-2
	Warrant Officer W-1
	Chief Master Sergeant of the Air Force
	Chief Master Sergeant
	Senior Master Sergeant
	Master Sergeant
	Technical Sergeant
	Staff Sergeant
	Airman First Class
	Airman Second Class
	Airman Third Class

Navy Departments led to his court martial (military trial) in 1925.

In 1926, the U.S. Air Service was reformed as the Army Air Corps. The Army's first B-17 bomber, known as the Flying Fortress, was built in 1935. It played a major role in the victory of the Allies in World War II. In 1941, the Army Air Forces (AAF) were organized under the command of General Henry H. "Hap" Arnold. Top strength of the AAF during the war was 2,400,000 members and almost 80,000 airplanes. In addition, the U.S. supplied thousands of planes to the Allies. In 1947, the U.S. Air Force was established as a separate military service. Since then, U.S.

▲ *The United States Air Force Academy is near Colorado Springs, Colorado. Opened in 1958, the Academy trains cadets wishing to become officers in the Air Force.*

warplanes have lifted vital supplies to West Berlin, flown combat missions in Korea and Vietnam, and helped maintain the peace around the world.

ALSO READ: AIRPLANE, ARMY, MISSILE, NAVY, WORLD WAR II.

AIRLINE An airline is a system that carries passengers and cargo through the air. Persons, mail, and freight can be rapidly transported by

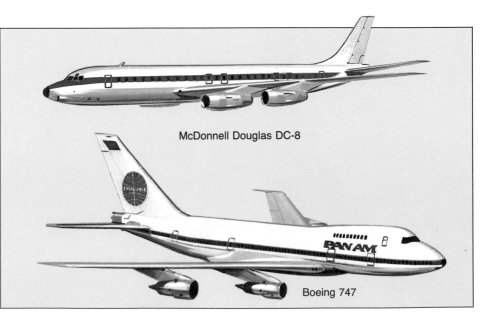

McDonnell Douglas DC-8

Boeing 747

airlines to almost any part of the world.

There are several kinds of airlines. The *commuter airlines* fly small planes that carry up to 20 people between small cities, or from small cities to larger ones. *Local airlines* fly between medium-sized cities or from medium-sized to large cities. Their planes may carry from 20 to 100 passengers. *Trunk airlines* usually fly between large cities within a country. Most of their airplanes are jets that carry from 100 to 300 people. *International flag carriers* fly big jets between the major cities of the world. These four kinds of airlines are called *scheduled air carriers*. They must fly at the times they advertise to the public, whether their airplanes are filled or not.

Cargo airlines carry freight instead of people. They fly fresh vegetables, fruits, and flowers to restaurants, grocery stores, and shops. They carry automobile parts, furniture, and animals for zoos. They deliver almost anything that needs to be delivered quickly and that requires careful handling. Cargo airlines use all kinds of airplanes, including the biggest jets.

Charter or *supplemental airlines* do not have schedules. They rent their airplanes and crews to clubs and other organizations, usually for vacation trips or meetings. The trips are usually planned six months before the flight, and all the passengers must go and come back together. Because a charter airline knows ahead of time that the airplane will be filled with passengers, the fare for each passenger is low. It is usually about half the cost of the same trip on a scheduled airline. Supplemental airlines fly the same big jets and have the same kinds of crews that the international scheduled airlines use.

Great changes have been made since the first airline flight. On January 1, 1914, a flying boat carried two passengers from Tampa to St. Petersburg in Florida. But air travel grew rapidly, especially after World War II. Today, millions of passengers are in the air, every year. They travel in comfort inside large airplanes such as the Boeing 747 which can carry more than 350 passengers for 6,000 miles (9,660 km) at 600 miles an hour (960 km/hr). It has a cocktail lounge and elevators to bring food up from the galley, or kitchen, to the cabin.

The first stewardess to serve on an airline was Ellen Church. She helped the passengers on a United Air Lines flight from San Francisco, California, to Cheyenne, Wyoming, on May 15, 1930.

▼ *On the flight deck of a modern airliner, the crew are aided by computers and other electronic instruments. The pilots sit side by side in the cockpit.*

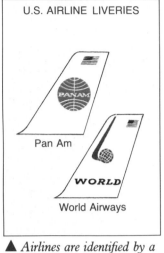

U.S. AIRLINE LIVERIES

Pan Am

WORLD

World Airways

▲ *Airlines are identified by a symbol on the vertical stabilizer.*

The first successful rocket-powered airplane was the German Me-163 *Komet* fighter. In 1944 it achieved a speed of over 500 mph (800 km/hr), with a very high rate of climb. But its fuel was used up in about 10 minutes.

▼ *The Wright brothers first flew in 1903. Their plane carried only one person at 30 miles an hour (about 50 km/hr). On its first flight, it flew just 120 feet (37 m).*

The People of an Airline The cockpit of an airliner is called the *flight deck*. The crew, or people who fly the airplane, includes the *captain*, the senior pilot who is in charge of the airplane, and usually another pilot called the *first officer*. The *flight engineer* is also a member of the flight crew. He is in charge of the mechanical operation of the airplane, which includes everything from the coffee makers to the engines. He watches all the meters and gauges in the cockpit and adjusts temperature, power, fuel, and other things to be sure everything is working right. On long overwater flights, the crew also includes a *navigator*. The navigator's job is to know where the airplane is at all times. He tells the pilot what route to follow and how long the trip should take.

The *cabin crew* of an airliner is made up of men and women called *flight attendants*. A Boeing 747 usually has about 15 flight attendants; smaller airplanes may have only two or three. Flight attendants serve food and are trained to take care of sick persons and to evacuate passengers quickly in case of an emergency. Many flight attendants speak several languages and can talk to passengers from different countries. Most of them have been to college. They are very important to airlines because not only do they help make the passengers' flight more pleasant, but they also make it safer.

The maintenance or engineering people take care of the airplanes on the ground. They are a very important part of the airline because they make sure that the airplanes are ready to fly safely.

Air travel has become so popular that every year the number of passengers who fly on world's scheduled airlines (not counting charter airlines and private planes) is larger than the total population of the United States.

ALSO READ: AIRPLANE, AIRPORT, AVIATION, TRANSPORTATION.

AIR MASS   see WEATHER.

AIRPLANE   On a lonely beach at Kitty Hawk, North Carolina, on December 17, 1903, a man flew an airplane for the first time. The man was Orville Wright. The flight was not far, only 120 feet (37 m). The airplane never got more than 20 feet (6 m) off the ground. Its top speed was only 30 miles an hour (50 km/hr). But, unlike earlier aircraft (such as balloons and gliders), it was an airplane—it flew under its own power and could be controlled by the pilot.

Aviation is today one of the world's largest industries. Orville and Wilbur Wright can be called the "fathers of aviation" because they were the first to design, build, and fly a successful engine-powered airplane.

The Wright brothers were good and careful mechanics. They tested small models of different types of wings before they built a full-size airplane. These models helped them understand the four basic forces that explain how an airplane flies.

Why an Airplane Flies The forces the Wrights discovered are called *lift*, *weight*, *thrust*, and *drag*. These forces work in the same way on a small model airplane, with a propeller driven by a rubber band, as they do on a giant transport plane driven by powerful jet engines.

Lift and weight are opposite forces. *Lift* makes an airplane go up, and *weight*—or *gravity*—makes it go

down. The lift must be stronger than the weight, if an airplane is to fly. Thrust and drag are also opposite forces. *Thrust* makes the airplane go forward or faster, and *drag* holds it back or slows it down. Thrust must be stronger than drag, for an airplane to take off.

To understand how these forces work on an airplane, you must look carefully at the airplane itself. The main parts of any airplane are the wings, the engine (or engines), the fuselage or cabin (the long part where the pilot and passengers or cargo ride), the landing gear (usually two large wheels or groups of wheels, and other parts to support an airplane on the ground), and the tail at the back.

LIFT. The movement of air around a wing creates lift. A wing of an airplane is curved on top and flat on the bottom. Air moving over the top must move faster than air moving under the bottom, because it has a longer distance to travel. The faster air travels, the less pressure it exerts. The air above the wing has a lower pressure than the air below. The higher pressure below forces the airplane up.

■ LEARN BY DOING

You can easily see how lift works. Tear a strip of paper, about 2 inches (5 cm) wide and 8 inches (20 cm) long, off a sheet of paper. Hold the strip at one end between your thumb and first finger so the long part hangs down over the back of your hand. Hold your hand near your mouth and blow across the top. The paper "wing" rises. If the paper were an airplane wing, the whole airplane would rise with it. ■

THRUST. The forward movement, or speed, of an airplane overcomes the drag of the air. A turning propeller pulls or pushes an airplane through air, much as a propeller pushes a motor boat through water. A jet engine works on the principle of

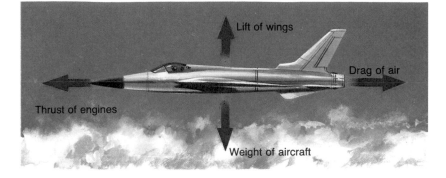

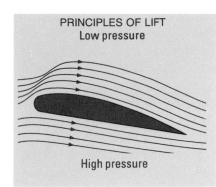

PRINCIPLES OF LIFT
Low pressure

High pressure

▲ *Four forces act on a plane in flight: lift and thrust (which move it upward and forward), and drag and weight (which move it backward and downward).*

◄ *An airplane wing tends to lift, because the air pressure beneath it is higher than the air pressure above it.*

reaction—the action of hot gases moving out the back of an engine causes a reaction of an airplane moving forward. If more thrust is supplied by the engine, more lift is created and an airplane can climb, or, if it is flying level, it can go faster.

WEIGHT. The weight of an airplane is the weight of the machine, plus cargo, passengers, and fuel. This force, which must be overcome by lift, is called *gravity*.

DRAG. The drag, or resistance, is caused by the friction of air on every part of the airplane. An airplane is going as fast as it can when as much drag as possible is overcome by

The airplane with the longest wingspan ever made was the Hughes Hercules flyingboat. It had a span of 320 feet (98 m) and weighed 190 tons (172 metric tons). In a test flight in 1947 its eight engines lifted it to a height of 70 feet (21 m) for a distance of 3,000 feet (914 m). It never flew again.

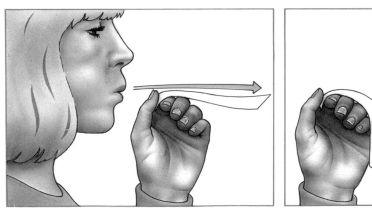

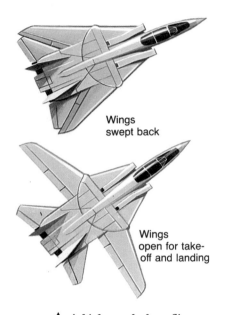

Wings
swept back

Wings
open for take-
off and landing

▲ *A high-speed plane flies faster if its wings are swept back. In a swing-wing design, the wings can be moved forward into the open position for take-off and landing.*

▲ *On a propeller-driven plane, the propellers pull the airplane forward against the drag of the air.*

thrust. Designers reduce the amount of drag by making the outside surfaces of the airplane as smooth and rounded as possible. The *landing gear* on most airplanes retracts, or pulls up, to reduce resistance during flight.

Other Parts of an Airplane   An airplane's *tail* has *horizontal stabilizers* that look like tiny wings on the tail. It also has a *vertical stabilizer* that sticks straight up from the middle of the tail. These parts keep an airplane balanced in flight and are called *control surfaces*. The *elevators* are attached to the horizontal stabilizers. A pilot can move these up or down and apply more or less power to make an airplane climb or descend.

The rudder is attached to the vertical stabilizer but (unlike a boat's rudder) is not normally used to steer the airplane. The rudder is used to stabilize the airplane while two movable sections near the wing tips, called *ailerons*, are used to turn the airplane to the left or right. To turn to the right, the pilot raises the right aileron and lowers the left aileron. This tips the right wing down and raises the left wing. The airplane then banks to the right and makes a slow, smooth turn. Other wing sections, near the fuselage, are called *flaps*. Flaps can be turned down to make the curve of the wing top greater. The increased pressure difference increases lift.

Many important parts of an airplane can be seen only in the *cockpit* where a pilot sits. In the cockpit are all the controls and electronic devices that enable a pilot to fly the airplane safely. The *flight controls* consist of a wheel or control stick, and rudder pedals. The wheel, which looks much like an automobile steering wheel, controls the elevators and ailerons. To make a right turn, a pilot turns the wheel to the right and pushes the right rudder pedal. If he pushes the wheel forward, the airplane descends. The airplane climbs if he pulls the wheel back.

Even on a small airplane a pilot has a number of dials, gauges, switches, and lights on an instrument panel that looks much like an automobile dashboard. On large airplanes, instrument panels cover the front, sides, and ceiling of the cockpit. The instruments tell a pilot everything he or she must know about how fast the plane is going, the direction it is flying, how much fuel is left, and many other things. Radar equipment shows the aircraft's position on its planned course. Radio equipment permits pilots to talk to people on the ground and to other airplanes. Ground radar and navigation beacons help pilots avoid storms and navigate their airplanes. *Automatic pilots* take over control from pilots on long flights.

Types of Airplanes   Three kinds of power systems are used today to furnish thrust. (1) Gasoline engines turn propellers that pull or push an airplane through the air. These airplanes are called *conventional aircraft*. They usually fly at speeds of 120 to 225 miles an hour (190–360 km/hr), but some can go faster. (2) Jet engines that turn propellers are called *turboprops*. Planes with such engines fly from 250 to 400 miles an hour (400–640 km/hr). (3) *Pure jet* engines push an airplane through the air at very high speeds—600 miles an hour (970 km/hr) or faster.

Most airplanes today are monoplanes, which means they have only one wing. In the early days of aviation, airplanes had two wings (biplanes) or three wings (triplanes). The extra wings added more lift, but also more drag. The lift was more than the drag, so the airplanes flew but could not go very fast. In very fast airplanes, the wings are often delta-shaped (like a triangle) or swept back in a V-shape.

ALSO READ: AIR FORCE, AIRLINE, AIRPORT, AVIATION, JET PROPULSION, TRANSPORTATION, WRIGHT BROTHERS.

Spoilers

Ailerons

Flaps

▶ The pilot has various controls to fly the airplane. Flaps and spoilers act like brakes. Ailerons are moved up and down to make the plane turn.

▲ An engineer checks a jet engine. Airline engines are regularly overhauled to keep them in good working condition.

▶ The landing gear of a DC-8 airliner. The wheels are lowered and the flaps are pushed down to create drag. The two sets of center wheels hit the runway first, followed by the nose wheel. The airplane then slows to a stop.

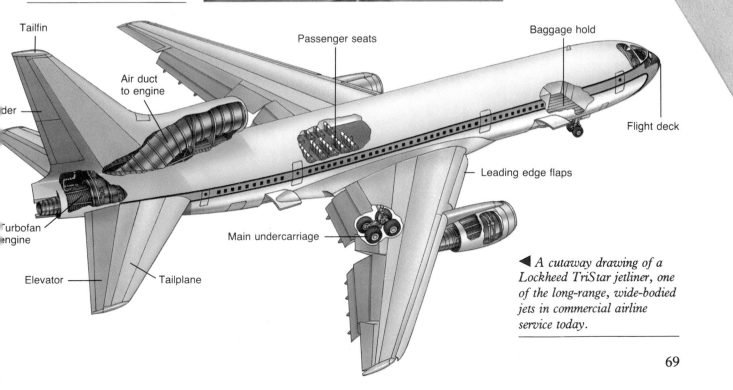

Tailfin

Air duct to engine

Passenger seats

Baggage hold

der

Flight deck

Leading edge flaps

Turbofan engine

Main undercarriage

Elevator

Tailplane

◀ A cutaway drawing of a Lockheed TriStar jetliner, one of the long-range, wide-bodied jets in commercial airline service today.

Famous Airplanes—1903-1918

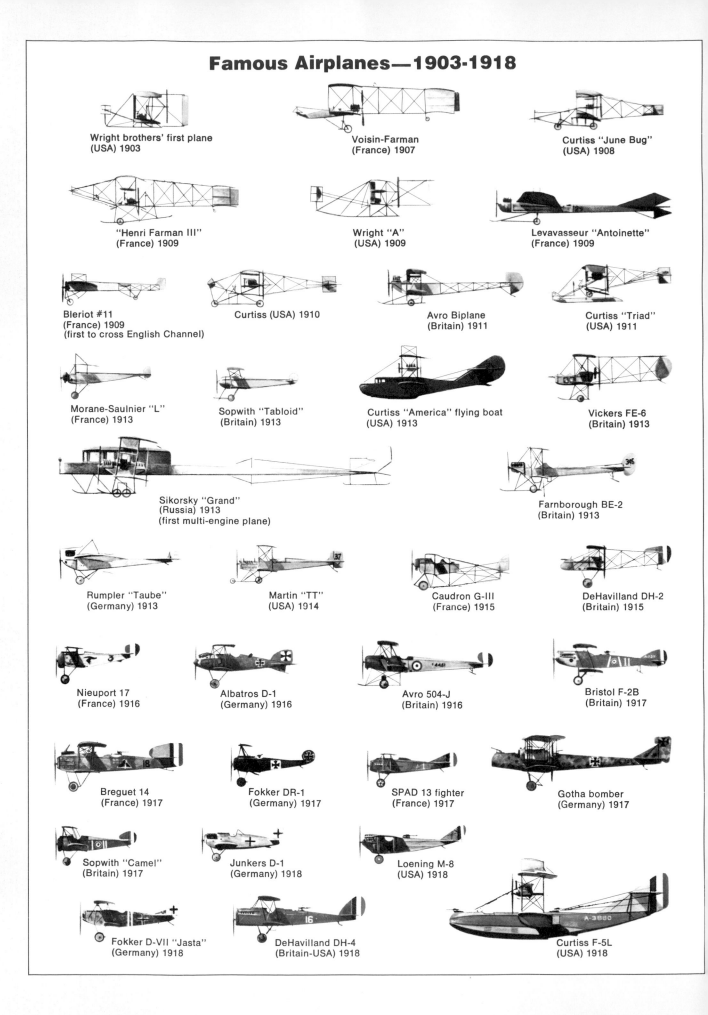

Wright brothers' first plane
(USA) 1903

Voisin-Farman
(France) 1907

Curtiss "June Bug"
(USA) 1908

"Henri Farman III"
(France) 1909

Wright "A"
(USA) 1909

Levavasseur "Antoinette"
(France) 1909

Bleriot #11
(France) 1909
(first to cross English Channel)

Curtiss (USA) 1910

Avro Biplane
(Britain) 1911

Curtiss "Triad"
(USA) 1911

Morane-Saulnier "L"
(France) 1913

Sopwith "Tabloid"
(Britain) 1913

Curtiss "America" flying boat
(USA) 1913

Vickers FE-6
(Britain) 1913

Sikorsky "Grand"
(Russia) 1913
(first multi-engine plane)

Farnborough BE-2
(Britain) 1913

Rumpler "Taube"
(Germany) 1913

Martin "TT"
(USA) 1914

Caudron G-III
(France) 1915

DeHavilland DH-2
(Britain) 1915

Nieuport 17
(France) 1916

Albatros D-1
(Germany) 1916

Avro 504-J
(Britain) 1916

Bristol F-2B
(Britain) 1917

Breguet 14
(France) 1917

Fokker DR-1
(Germany) 1917

SPAD 13 fighter
(France) 1917

Gotha bomber
(Germany) 1917

Sopwith "Camel"
(Britain) 1917

Junkers D-1
(Germany) 1918

Loening M-8
(USA) 1918

Fokker D-VII "Jasta"
(Germany) 1918

DeHavilland DH-4
(Britain-USA) 1918

Curtiss F-5L
(USA) 1918

Famous Airplanes—1919-first jets

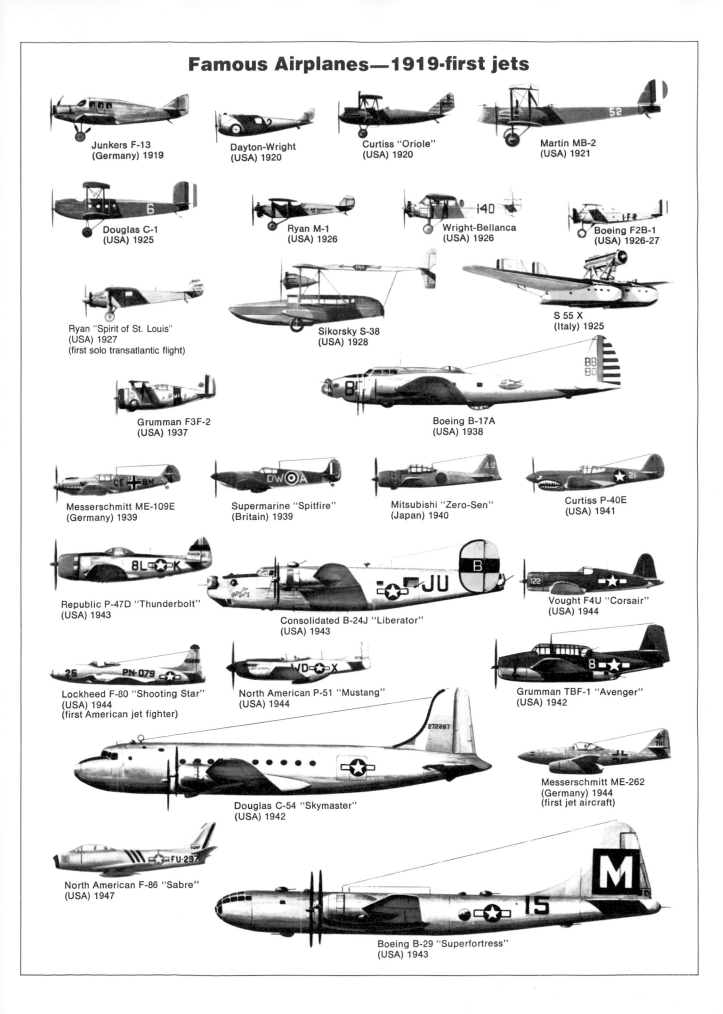

Junkers F-13
(Germany) 1919

Dayton-Wright
(USA) 1920

Curtiss "Oriole"
(USA) 1920

Martin MB-2
(USA) 1921

Douglas C-1
(USA) 1925

Ryan M-1
(USA) 1926

Wright-Bellanca
(USA) 1926

Boeing F2B-1
(USA) 1926-27

Ryan "Spirit of St. Louis"
(USA) 1927
(first solo transatlantic flight)

Sikorsky S-38
(USA) 1928

S 55 X
(Italy) 1925

Grumman F3F-2
(USA) 1937

Boeing B-17A
(USA) 1938

Messerschmitt ME-109E
(Germany) 1939

Supermarine "Spitfire"
(Britain) 1939

Mitsubishi "Zero-Sen"
(Japan) 1940

Curtiss P-40E
(USA) 1941

Republic P-47D "Thunderbolt"
(USA) 1943

Consolidated B-24J "Liberator"
(USA) 1943

Vought F4U "Corsair"
(USA) 1944

Lockheed F-80 "Shooting Star"
(USA) 1944
(first American jet fighter)

North American P-51 "Mustang"
(USA) 1944

Grumman TBF-1 "Avenger"
(USA) 1942

Douglas C-54 "Skymaster"
(USA) 1942

Messerschmitt ME-262
(Germany) 1944
(first jet aircraft)

North American F-86 "Sabre"
(USA) 1947

Boeing B-29 "Superfortress"
(USA) 1943

AIR POLLUTION A large city, even on a warm sunny day, may sometimes be covered by a hazy mist, or even by a dense gray cloud. The mist is dirty, or *polluted* air. The cloud is *smog*—a mixture of smoke and fog—an especially unpleasant kind of air pollution. Smog is harmful. It often causes shortness of breath, dizziness, watery eyes, and runny noses. Smog can also be dangerous if it is extra thick and lasts a long time. In the days when people burned coal for cooking and heating and in factory furnaces, cities were often shrouded in smoke.

Wind carries many substances through Earth's air. Among them are pollen from plants, sand from dry beaches, and dust from fields. These are natural substances. But humans add other substances to the air. Smoke pours from factory smokestacks. Chemical fumes rise from paper mills and metal-working plants. Garbage-dump incinerators spread black soot. Automobiles stream a blue, smelly haze that hangs over crowded cities. The air is polluted when it is filled with unnatural substances.

What Pollution Can Do Polluted air can destroy the balance of the exchange that goes on among plants, animals, and the oceans. Animals, including people, get the oxygen they need from the air they breathe. They exhale (breathe out) the gas carbon dioxide. Plants, even those that live in the oceans, all need carbon dioxide as much as people need oxygen. Carbon dioxide supplies the carbon that plants need to make food. Plants draw in carbon dioxide, then release oxygen. But *pollutants* such as soot, sulfur, lead, and automobile exhaust and factory fumes poison the air.

◀ *Smoke and gas are poured into the atmosphere by oilfields, factories, cities, automobiles, and power stations.*

Over a long period of time, these pollutants could poison all forms of life.

Air pollution causes other serious problems, too. Foul air damages crops. Air pollution wears away (*corrodes*) metals as though they had been put into acid. Layers of ash and soot from air settle on buildings and clothing, and cleaning costs rise. People cannot see clearly in heavy smog, so accidents happen more often. Fumes in the air even eat away buildings made of stone. Pollutants cause holes in glass and kill lawns and trees. Polluted air can also cause a health threat, especially to people with breathing problems.

Pollutants from industrial plants, such as steelworks and chemical factories, can be carried by the wind many hundreds of miles. The chemicals in this dirty air can fall back to Earth as another form of pollution, *acid rain*.

Take a Deep Breath Almost 1,000 tons (910 metric tons) of soot and ash land on every square mile (2.5 sq. km) of New York City each year. The 125 million cars that Americans own add large amounts of poisonous carbon monoxide (from their engines) to the air every day. Each year more factories are built, more fuel is burned to provide power and heat, more people drive cars.

The most serious fact about air pollution is that it endangers health. Eyes water and vision blurs. A person may not get the oxygen he needs when he breathes. He may choke on harmful gases instead. Old people, and people with heart or lung diseases, suffer most from polluted air.

People of all ages have become aware of the danger of air pollution today, and they are working to stop it. The United States Government formed the Environmental Protection Agency in 1970. This office studies pollution and works with people all over the U.S. to prevent further pollution of the air.

Automobile makers must now produce engines that give off less pollutants. To meet U.S. federal standards, most new cars have special pollution control devices, called *catalytic converters*. These clean up some of the poisonous gases from the car's engine. Automobile makers have begun to develop electric-powered cars, which do not cause air pollution. Jet airplanes have devices that cut down the dirty black clouds of jet fuel exhaust. Los Angeles has a city law to shut factories when there is danger of heavy smog. Many cities no longer allow people to burn trash or leaves.

The Greenhouse Effect Some scientists believe that one effect of the air pollution caused by human activities

▲ *This wind-power electricity generator in Denmark causes no air pollution.*

Air pollution throughout the United States is slowly increasing. But in dozens of U.S. cities the air is actually cleaner than it was 15 years ago. In 1970 the average city dweller breathed unsafe air for almost 70 days in the year. That figure is now down to less than 40 days.

DANGEROUS POLLUTANTS

SMOKE: People complained about smoke from coal fires as early as the 1200's.

SULFUR GAS: Comes from burning coal and oil.

HYDROCARBONS: A dangerous hydrocarbon is carbon monoxide gas, from automobile engines' unburned fuel.

NITROGEN OXIDES: From automobiles, power plants, and factory boilers. They combine with hydrocarbons to form photochemicals—one of the causes of smog.

PARTICULATES: Such as dust, grit, and soot.

ACIDS: May fall as acid rain, when chemicals combine with water in the air.

LEAD: From automobiles using old-style, unleaded gasoline.

RADIOACTIVE MATERIAL: Comes from nuclear waste and nuclear accidents.

OTHER DANGEROUS SUBSTANCES: Include ammonia, chloroform, vinyl chloride, ethylene oxide, asbestos, mercury, and benzene.

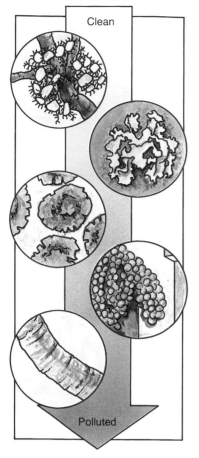

Clean

Polluted

▲ *Air pollution affects living things. Lichens thrive in clean air, but cannot live in polluted air.*

One of the main causes of air pollution is the gasoline engine. Automobile manufacturers are trying to reduce the pollution from vehicle exhausts, but the only real answer may be the development of new kinds of engines driven by steam, hydrogen, or electricity.

▶ *Chemicals in polluted air eat into the surface of stone buildings and statues. Historic buildings need to be protected if their stonework is to survive hundreds more years.*

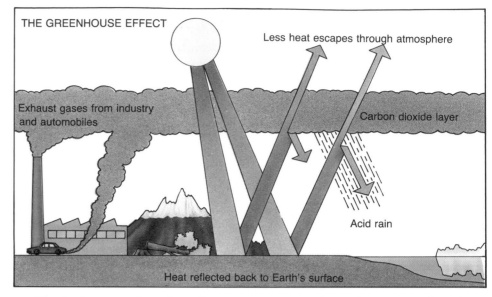

THE GREENHOUSE EFFECT

Less heat escapes through atmosphere

Exhaust gases from industry and automobiles

Carbon dioxide layer

Acid rain

Heat reflected back to Earth's surface

on Earth is to make the climate warmer. They call this the "greenhouse effect." This is how they think it works.

From the exhausts of automobiles and the smoke from factory smokestacks, carbon dioxide gas is released into the atmosphere. This gas forms a kind of blanket around Earth. Heat from the sun, which warms Earth, normally escapes into space. But as the amount of carbon dioxide in the atmosphere grows, more of this heat is trapped. The polluted atmosphere begins to act just like the glass in a greenhouse. As Earth warms up, more water vapor forms, and this too

prevents heat from escaping into space.

The "greenhouse effect" could have good results. It could make the cold, dry areas of Earth warmer and wetter, and better for agriculture. But it could also cause problems. Areas that are mild and fertile today could become too hot for the kind of agriculture carried on there today. Clouds could blot out the sunlight needed to ripen crops. If Earth got too warm, the glaciers and ice caps of polar regions would melt more freely. This extra water would run into the seas, and the rising sea level could flood low-lying land. No one knows for sure about the results of the "greenhouse effect." But most scientists agree that we must do our best to clean up the air, and prevent further pollution.

To solve the air pollution problem, scientists in the U.S., Europe, and Japan have begun to develop cleaner alternative energy sources, such as solar heat, wind, and wave power. They are concerned about the long term effect of air pollution on people and the environment.

■ LEARN BY DOING

Many newspapers print a *pollution index* each day. It usually shows whether the air was "good," "poor," or "unacceptable" during the day.

(The terms used in your paper may be different.) Follow the changes in the pollution index for your town. Make a chart with six columns. Label the columns "Day," "Sunny," "Cloudy," "Rain," "Wind Speed," and "Pollution Index." Fill in the chart each day for several weeks. Do you see a pattern developing? When is the pollution index "unacceptable"? When is it "good"? ■

ALSO READ: ACID RAIN, BREATHING, CONSERVATION, ECOLOGY, WATER POLLUTION.

AIRPORT An airport is a place where an airplane can take off and land safely. A simple airport may be just a piece of smooth ground. But ground gets muddy, so most airports, even far from cities, have runways. These are usually made of concrete or asphalt, like highways. But they are wider and thicker than highways. Runways are built following the most frequent wind directions. A small airport is usually owned by a person or a town. It is run by a *fixed-base operator* who provides the basic services needed at all airports. These include "parking lots" for the airplanes, taxiways (roads) to the main runway, fuel supplies, weather information and maps for the pilots, and mechanics to make repairs. Many fixed-base operators also give flying lessons.

Small airports can be as important as larger ones. Some small airports are the center of areas called *industrial air parks*. The airport itself is surrounded by factories and other businesses that need swift transportation. It helps the local community by serving manufacturers as well as privately owned aircraft.

The Large Airports Large airports in cities have two main types of customers—the airlines and the passengers. For the airlines, airports have maintenance services in huge build-

ings, called *hangars*. Airplanes can be parked in the hangars and worked on in any kind of weather, day or night, by expert mechanics. The mechanics make sure the airplanes are safe to fly. Communications services at airports include the control towers, where air traffic controllers watch the airports and tell pilots when to land or take off, and which of several runways to use. Landing and navigation aids, which are radio and radar stations, help pilots to find the airports and to land in bad weather. Airport weather services tell pilots what the weather is anywhere in the world, and what it will be like when they arrive at their destinations. Inflight food services furnish food for passengers in airplanes. Air cargo warehouses are big buildings where cargo is stored between flights.

An important job of the people who run airports is to keep airplanes safely going and coming in bad weather. Runways must be maintained so that rainwater quickly drains away. In winter snowplows keep the runways clear of snow. The light and radar aids on runways must always be ready to help pilots in darkness or fog. Airports often do such a

▲ *The departure lounge of a Japanese airport. Airport design aims to provide comfort and security for travelers.*

▼ *Landing lights on the airport runway guide incoming aircraft.*

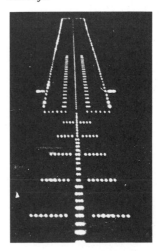

▲ *Typical layout of a modern airport.*

Two of the world's largest airports are in Saudi Arabia. They are named after kings. The King Abdul-Aziz airport, at Jeddah, opened in 1981. The even larger King Khaled airport, at Riyadh, opened in 1983. The Jeddah airport receives Muslim pilgrims journeying to Mecca, and its marble buildings are designed to look like Arab nomads' tents.

good job that airplanes keep flying after ground transportation has been almost halted by bad weather.

Each airline has ground services including people who check passengers' tickets, check in passengers' luggage, and announce arrivals and departures of planes. The skycaps who carry passengers' luggage, and the people who fill airplanes with fuel, are also part of the ground services. At large airports, passengers wait in lounges in the passenger terminal buildings before they get on the airplanes. They also go into these buildings when they get off at their destinations. The passenger terminal buildings have ticket counters, restrooms, telephones, barber shops, restaurants, drug stores, and various shops.

Some large airports are *international*

airports, where flights go to and from other countries. These airports have United States officials who check all arriving passengers to see if they are legally allowed to enter the U.S. and to see if passengers are bringing into the country things they should not. Flights across oceans use very large airplanes that need much runway space, so international airports are usually very large. Dulles International Airport, near Washington, D.C., is an example. It is about 4 miles (6 km) wide and 5 miles (8 km) long. It has four runways, the longest ones 11,500 feet (3,505 m) long, and 150 feet (45 m) wide.

International airports are very busy, because they handle not only overseas flights but domestic flights as well. Some have flights of more than 50 airlines arriving and leaving each

▲ *Electronic scanners check air passengers' baggage and bodies, to ensure safety in the air.*

day. The busiest airport in the world is Chicago's O'Hare International. On a busy day, an airplane takes off or lands there about every 43 seconds. The world's second busiest airport is Atlanta's Hartsfield International, followed by Los Angeles International, London's Heathrow, and New York's Kennedy International.

Take-offs and landings of jet airplanes have caused problems of noise control. New airports are being built away from populated areas.

ALSO READ: AIRLINE, AIRPLANE, AIR TRAFFIC CONTROL, AVIATION.

AIR PRESSURE Air is not very heavy. One cubic foot (.03 m³) of air at sea level, and at 32° F (0°C), weighs only one ounce (28 g), which is about the weight of eight pennies. So much air is in the *atmosphere* above and around us that it presses on us from all directions with a pressure, or weight, of almost 15 pounds per square inch (1.1 kg/cm²) at sea level. The air pressure on our bodies amounts to thousands of pounds. We are not generally aware of this great force because the fluid and air in our bodies are pushing out with an equal pressure.

The air above just one acre (4,047 sq. m) of ground weighs over 40,000

tons (36,287 metric tons). The weight of air is only half as much 4 miles (6 km) above Earth. At 15,000 feet (4,500 m) above Earth the air is thinner and contains less oxygen than at ground level. A pilot must wear an oxygen mask unless his plane is pressurized and has oxygen supplies. Passenger airplanes are pressurized, to keep the cabin pressure much like that of ground level.

An instrument called a *barometer* measures atmospheric pressure. Knowledge of air pressure is very useful in predicting the weather. High air pressure usually means fair weather. If air pressure is low, stormy weather is likely.

Air pressure can be put to work. When air is *compressed*, or squeezed together, in a small space, it rushes out through any opening with great force. A tool called a *pneumatic hammer*, or drill, uses the force of compressed air to drive the hammer deep into concrete, breaking it up.

■ **LEARN BY DOING**
Test the pressure of the air yourself, using a bowl of water, a glass, and a napkin. Fill a deep bowl with water. Crush a paper napkin and force it tightly into the bottom of the glass. Turn the glass upside down and push it straight down into the water. Now pull the glass straight out. Feel the napkin. It should be dry. The air that was inside the glass when it was

▲ *A vacuum is created inside a can when all the air inside is pumped out. The outside air pressure will then cause the can to crumple (bottom).*

◄ *A great deal of air can be compressed into small tanks. These divers are checking their air tanks. They will wear the tanks under water and breathe air from them.*

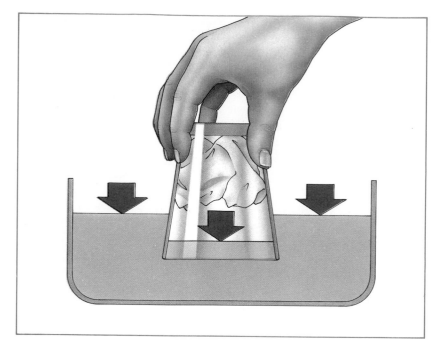

ship aloft. Rigid airships remain the same shape, even if there is no gas inside them. They are sometimes called *dirigibles*, from a French word for "steerable." They are also called *zeppelins*, after Count Ferdinand von Zeppelin of Germany, who designed the first rigid airships that worked well.

Non-rigid airships are called *blimps*. Blimps do not have a complete inside frame. They depend on the pressure of the gas inside to keep them inflated to their normal shape. They may have a number of separate gas sections so that a gas leak in one section will not cause the blimp to come down suddenly. Non-rigid airships are the kind most often seen today.

pushed into the water had enough pressure, or force, to keep water from filling the glass. ■

ALSO READ: AIR, AIRPLANE, ATMOSPHERE, WEATHER.

▼ *The age of flight dawned in 1783 when two Frenchmen rose into the air in a hot-air balloon, invented by the Montgolfier brothers.*

AIRSHIP You may have seen an occasional airship overhead—half-floating, half-gliding through the sky like a giant silver cigar. It is a huge "balloon" filled with lighter-than-air gas to make it rise. A balloon has no engines. It must travel wherever the wind takes it. In the 1800's inventors tried fitting engines into balloons. They made the first airships. An airship has engines to move it through the sky and controls to steer it by.

There are two main types of airships—*rigid* and *non-rigid*. Rigid airships have a "skeleton" or framework of aluminum or some other lightweight but strong material. The frame is covered with a tightly stretched skin of cloth or some other fabric. Lightweight metal is sometimes used instead of cloth to cover the frame. A number of bags of light gas are inside the frame. If one bag breaks or leaks, the others keep the

Development of the Airship Henri Giffard of France in 1852 flew a long sausage-shaped balloon filled with hydrogen, for 17 miles (27 km) at 5 miles an hour (8 km/hr). He used a 3½-horsepower steam engine to turn a big three-bladed propeller for power, and used a boat rudder to steer. Other airship pioneers tried other ways of developing power, including electricity. However, none of these early airships worked very well until the lightweight gasoline engine was invented. The Brazilian Alberto Santos-Dumont flew a number of gasoline-engined airships in the early 1900's.

Count von Zeppelin had four airships flying passengers between German cities by 1910. German zeppelins bombed London in World War I. However, British airplanes soon proved it was easy to shoot down the huge, slow airships.

The Age of the Airship The high point in airship history came in 1929, when the German *Graf Zeppelin* flew around the world in 21 days. It had a crew of 40 and carried 20 passengers. The huge silver airship was 776 feet (237 m) long, and flew 80 miles an hour (129 km/hr). The *Graf Zeppelin* started its famous flight in Lakehurst, New Jersey. It landed only three times, first in Friedrichshafen, Germany, next in Tokyo, Japan. It then flew over the Pacific Ocean to Los Angeles, California. From there it returned to Lakehurst. The *Graf Zeppelin* flew safely for nine years, and carried a total of more than 18,000 passengers.

Encouraged by the success of the *Graf Zeppelin*, the Germans built the *Hindenburg*. The *Hindenburg* was the largest rigid airship ever built—803 feet (245 m) long and twice as fat as the *Graf Zeppelin*. It carried 78 passengers and 19 crew members. It made ten successful round trips between Germany and the United States in 1936. But, on May 6, 1937, the hydrogen gas inside it exploded and the *Hindenburg* crashed as it was landing at Lakehurst. Of the 97 people on board, 36 were killed and the rest were badly injured. This tragedy ended the age of the airship. The British had lost their *R-101* airship in 1930, and with the *Hindenburg* disaster Germany too abandoned lighter-than-air craft.

Many accidents to European airships were caused by explosions of the hydrogen gas used to lift them. Hydrogen burns easily. U.S. airships used helium, a gas almost as light as hydrogen, but which will not burn. The U.S. has most of the world's helium supply. Germany had none for its zeppelins and so had to use hydrogen.

Between 1920 and 1935, the U.S. Navy built three huge dirigibles—the *Shenandoah*, the *Macon*, and the *Akron*. The *Macon* and the *Akron* each carried five small airplanes that could take off and land from the airship in flight. All three airships eventually crashed: *Shenandoah* in 1925, *Akron* in 1932, *Macon* in 1935. They were not strong enough to fly in bad weather.

One type of airship that worked successfully was the U.S. Navy blimp. Ten of these were used in World War II on antisubmarine patrols and to escort 80,000 U.S. ships across the ocean.

Today, there is new interest in airships, and better ways of building them. Airships move so slowly and calmly that they are useful for shooting television pictures from above, for a "bird's eye view" of important news events. In the future, airships could provide cheap transportation and also popular sightseeing flights. The age of the airship could return.

ALSO READ: AVIATION, BALLOON.

▲ *The* Hindenburg *exploded while landing at Lakehurst, New Jersey, in 1937. This tragedy halted airship development.*

The German Airship Transportation Company was the world's first airline. From 1910 to 1914, it carried more than 35,000 passengers between various cities in Germany. Though there were some accidents, not one person was killed.

◄ *Blimps contain no solid structure. This is the blimp* Mayflower *built by Goodyear.*

▲ Air-traffic controllers make sure that airplanes take off and land safely, and warn the pilots by radio if two planes get near one another. From the airport control tower, they watch all local air traffic on their radar screens.

Most airplanes nowadays have automatic landing equipment. The pilot sets the speed for touchdown and a computer does the rest. It adjusts all the controls and throttles automatically.

AIR TRAFFIC CONTROL The traffic police of the air is air traffic control (ATC). This control system directs airplanes somewhat as the police direct cars. It keeps airplanes from running into each other by telling them when to turn, how high and fast to fly, and when to land. Air highways in some areas are almost as crowded with airplanes as highways on the ground are crowded with automobiles. Different kinds of airplanes fly at different speeds, too. Some small airplanes fly at about 120 miles an hour (190 km/hr). Airliners can fly at 600 miles an hour (960 km/hr). Some military airplanes fly more than 1,200 miles an hour (1,900 km/hr). Dozens of airplanes may be flying over an area at the same time. All have to share the sky in safety.

Radar is a device that allows air traffic controllers to "observe" an airplane as a blip of light on a screen. The blip moves as the airplane moves. Two-way radio lets the controllers talk to the pilot of a plane. Air traffic controllers use these two main ways to keep track of all air traffic in their area.

The highways of the sky are called *airways*. The airways are run from *air route traffic control centers*. The control centers are in big buildings equipped with radar screens, powerful radios, computers, and many telephones. Each controller is in charge of all the airplanes flying in one *sector*, or area. When an airplane is about to leave this sector, the controller "hands it over" (by radio) to the controller of the next sector. The controller then tells the pilot to tune his radio to the new controller's frequency.

ATC provides *separation* between airplanes to keep traffic moving smoothly, quickly, and safely. This separation is like keeping all trucks and cars in separate lanes on a highway. Airplanes must be kept apart in three directions—up and down, side to side, and forward and behind.

When one airplane is flying above another, it must stay at least 1,000 feet higher (300 m). Controllers help keep these distances by assigning *altitudes*, or *flight levels*, to each airplane. Above 18,000 feet (5,400 m)—where the big, fast passenger jets fly—airplanes are kept 2,000 feet (600 m) apart. When they are side by side, airplanes must keep at a safe distance away from each other. Also, airplanes must usually be kept at least ten minutes' flying time from the airplanes in front and behind that are at the same altitude. In order to speed traffic, controllers may at times reduce the forward-and-behind distance to five minutes when they can see all the airplanes in their sectors on their radar screens.

Powerful radar stations along the airways send up *signal patterns* in the shape of a cone, with the small end at ground level. There are enough radar stations along the continental United States airways, so that the cones overlap above 24,000 feet (7,200 m) and all high-flying aircraft can be seen. At lower altitudes, planes may fly in spaces that the controllers cannot see on their radar screens. So pilots must make *position reports* over their radios. The pilots tell the controllers at what time they are over the stations, and their altitudes and speeds. A pilot is told to slow down, or hold, if his plane gets too close to an airplane in front of him. To *hold* means to circle the station until the traffic ahead is cleared.

Traffic jams happen at big airports, where different kinds of airplanes are coming in to land from all directions. As soon as they are within 30 miles (50 km) of an airport, all planes must call the *airport traffic control tower*. The control tower takes over from the air route traffic control center. The tower has special radar equipment that can detect all airplanes at all altitudes. The controller in the tower tells each pilot when to land and which runway to use.

The control tower is also in charge of the radar and radio landing aids at the airport. These are called *precision approach radar* (PAR) and *instrument landing systems* (ILS). A trained pilot can safely land an airplane by using them, just by looking at the instruments in the airplane cockpit. In bad weather or at night, a pilot may not be able to see the runway until he is only 100 feet (30 m) above it. But with PAR and ILS, he can still land safely. In fact, the most modern planes can land themselves, without a pilot, in an emergency.

Air traffic control works the same way all over the world. Air traffic control in the United States is run by the Federal Aviation Administration (FAA), which is part of the U.S. Department of Transportation.

ALABAMA When Alabama was Indian country, the Alibamu tribe lived along one of its rivers. The name *Alibamu* meant "I clear land." These Indians made clearings in the forest. In the clearings, they raised corn, squash, and beans. White settlers gradually turned *Alibamu* into *Alabama*. The state later took this name.

Alabama is in the Deep South. It is bordered on the west by the state of Mississippi, on the east by Georgia,

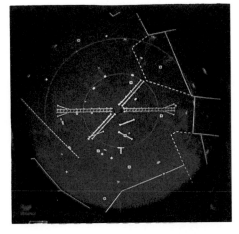

◀ *Radar shows the ground controllers where every plane is, and in which direction it is heading. Each plane shows as dots of light, or blips, on the radar screen.*

on the north by Tennessee, and on the south by Florida and the Gulf of Mexico.

The Land Nature has divided the state into two natural parts. One part, northeastern Alabama, is high and hilly. It belongs to the great Appalachian Highland. Trails used for hiking and riding twist through the hills. There are waterfalls and caves to visit and lakes for fishing and swimming. Beautiful flowers and shrubs brighten the woods. Farms here have always been small because the land is not very good.

The rest of Alabama is part of the Gulf Coastal Plain. The plain is low. In some places, it is almost flat. In others, it is gently rolling. More than half of Alabama is in the coastal plain. Not all of this part is good for farming. Some land is swampy. Some has poor soil. Pine woods cover much of the poorer land. Bald cypress trees grow in the swamps, with gray streamers of Spanish moss hanging from their branches.

Alabama's coastal plain has much good soil. The very best lies in the Black Belt. This strip curves through central Alabama. It is one of the most fertile areas in the world. The soil that gave the belt its name is dark because thickly growing plants decayed in it for thousands of years. Summers are long and hot in Alabama. Winters are mild. There is usually plenty of rain. Farmers like the climate.

▼ *In Alabama, the owners of cotton plantations often had very large houses. This one in Mobile was built in 1830. It is now a museum.*

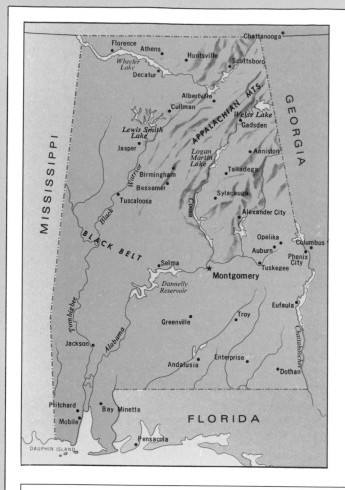

ALABAMA

Capital
Montgomery (185,000 people)

Area
51,609 square miles (133,657 sq. km)
Rank: 29th

Population
4,021,000 people. Rank: 22nd

Statehood
December 14, 1819 (22nd state admitted)

Principal river
Mobile River (formed by Tombigbee and Alabama rivers)

Highest point
Cheaha Mountain 2,407 feet (734 m)

Largest city
Birmingham (280,000 people)

Famous people
George Washington Carver, Hellen Keller.

Motto
Andemus Jura Nostra Defendere ("We Dare Defend Our Rights")

Song
"Alabama"

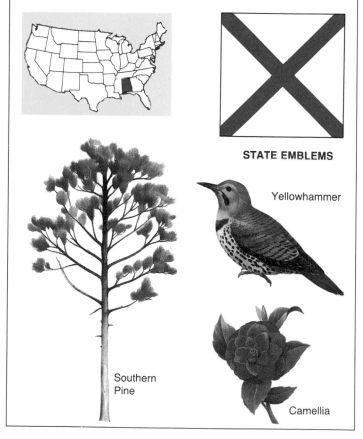

STATE EMBLEMS

Yellowhammer

Southern Pine

Camellia

▲ *An impressive display of rockets at the Huntsville Space Center, Alabama.*

History Among the Indians of Alabama were the Creeks, Chickasaws, Choctaws, and Cherokees. The Indians saw first Spaniards, then Frenchmen and Englishmen arrive in their territory. After the American Revolution, the land was given up by the British and became part of the United States. The government made the Indians give up their hunting grounds. Most of them were moved to reservations.

New settlers, spurred by the end of Indian troubles, poured into the region. The whites were mainly farmers; the blacks were their slaves. In 1817, the Territory of Alabama was formed; two years later it became a state.

White men who could not afford to buy fertile bottomlands settled in the uplands. They made a poor living cultivating the stony fields. Wealthy white men established large farms called *plantations* in the bottomlands. The plantation owners, planters, grew cotton in the rich soil. They raised so much that Alabama became known as the "Cotton State." The slave-owning planters grew richer and dominated Alabama. The black men, women, and children who worked in the fields earned nothing.

Alabama left the Union in 1861 and joined the Confederate States of America. Alabama's capital, Montgomery, was also the capital of the Confederacy until the Confederate government moved to Richmond, Virginia. The Civil War ended in defeat for the Confederate States. All slaves were freed. Workers had to be paid. Although they were offered very little, most blacks went back to the cotton fields because they had no other way to earn a living.

It was bad for Alabama to rely on just cotton. The black field hands never made a good living raising it. Neither did white farmers whose farms were small. And in some years, cotton did not sell very well. Such years were hard for everyone, even

▲ *Beautiful gardens abound in Alabama. This one is part of Bellingrath Gardens near Mobile.*

the plantation owners. By planting only one crop, they allowed cotton to wear out the soil.

An insect, the boll weevil, helped save Alabama and the rest of the South. It destroyed so much cotton every year that farmers began raising a number of other crops. Alabama no longer depends on cotton. In the town square of Enterprise, Alabama, stands a monument honoring the boll weevil!

During the 1880's, business owners began building factories in Alabama. The wages they paid were not high. But factories gave some Alabamians a better living than they could earn on farms. As manufacturing grew, wages were raised.

The poorest people of the state were the blacks. But they, too, made progress. Black leaders appeared in Alabama. One was Booker T. Washington. Born a Virginia slave, he built Tuskegee Institute for the education of blacks. At the institute is the workshop of the Missouri-born black scientist, George Washington Carver.

People from Alabama have contributed much to the world. William Gorgas, a U.S. Army doctor, helped stop yellow fever, a disease that almost prevented the building of the

Since Alabama became a state in 1819 it has had five different capitals: St. Stephens, Huntsville, Cahaba, Tuscaloosa, and Montgomery.

▲ *Alabama's Capitol Building in Montgomery.*

Panama Canal. Helen Keller, who as a baby was made deaf and blind by a serious illness, learned to communicate with others. The example of her courage has helped many handicapped people. Georgia-born Martin Luther King, Jr., went from being a minister in Montgomery to winner of the Nobel Peace Prize for his work in civil rights. And scientists at an Alabama university discovered a new chemical element, francium.

Alabamians at Work The nickname "Cotton State" no longer fits Alabama. Farmers earn more from broiler chickens, cattle, eggs, and milk products than from cotton and all other field crops put together. Much cotton is still grown, but today more land is planted in corn than in cotton. Soybeans, peanuts, and pecans are also major crops.

Agriculture has today lost its first place to manufacturing. Metal production is the leading type of manufacturing. The Birmingham area is the biggest iron-and-steel center in the South. On top of Red Mountain, overlooking Birmingham, is a tall statue of Vulcan, the Roman god of fire and metalworking. Other products are textiles, chemicals, paper goods, and food.

Manufacturing is aided by Alabama's raw materials. Coal is burned to make iron and steel and to produce electricity, too. Stone is used for building and for making cement. Gas-

oline, oil, and other products come from petroleum. Timber is made into lumber and paper.

Fishing is important to Alabama. Alabamians haul in several million dollars' worth of seafood every year. Crabs and oysters are taken from Mobile Bay. Boats go out into the Gulf of Mexico for shrimp, sardines, and other fish. Mobile Bay is also a major seaport. Goods from all over the South are shipped around the world from Mobile.

The Space Age brought a new kind of work to Alabama. In 1960 the National Aeronautics and Space Administration (NASA) opened a flight center at Huntsville. Scientists and engineers came there to work on rockets for space flight. They developed the mighty Saturn 5 Rocket that sent Americans to the moon.

ALSO READ: CARVER, GEORGE WASHINGTON; CIVIL RIGHTS; CIVIL WAR; KELLER, HELEN; KING, MARTIN LUTHER, JR.; WASHINGTON, BOOKER T.

ALAMO "Remember the Alamo!" was the Texans' battle cry during their fight for independence from Mexico. Often called the "Cradle of Texas Liberty," the fort of the Alamo in San Antonio was built as the Mission San Antonio de Valero in 1718 by Spanish missionaries. The mission-fortress was later nicknamed "Alamo," the Spanish word for "cottonwood," because of the cottonwoods around it.

San Antonio was part of Mexico in 1835. But Americans living there decided to rebel. A small group of Texas volunteers, led by William Travis, took over the Alamo in late December. Davy Crockett and Jim Bowie, the famous frontiersmen, were among them.

The Mexican General Santa Anna surrounded the Alamo with over 4,000 troops on February 23, 1836.

▼ *Remember the Alamo! In 1836, Texans fought for their freedom from Mexico at the old mission fort called the Alamo.*

All the 150 fighting men in the fort, plus 32 volunteers, refused to surrender. Against such overwhelming odds, they held out for 13 days until the last man was killed. The only survivors were two women and two children.

This heroic resistance aroused all Texans. Sam Houston led Texas forces to victory against General Santa Anna six weeks later, and Texas won its independence. Many years later, the Alamo was restored as an historic site and memorial.

ALSO READ: BOWIE, JIM; CROCKETT, DAVY; HOUSTON, SAM; TEXAS.

ALARIC (about A.D. 370–410) A group of people called the *Goths* lived in the fourth century. The Goths were divided into two branches, the eastern *Ostrogoths* and the western *Visigoths*. Alaric was king of the Visigoths.

Alaric was born on the island of Peuce in the Danube River, now in Romania. The Roman emperor gave him an army in 394. The next year the Visigoths elected Alaric king. He wanted more power. He tried first, unsuccessfully, to conquer Greece,

▼ *Alaric was the warrior king of the ancient Visigoths.*

and then turned against Rome.

The Visigoths entered Italy several times to attack Rome. In 408 and 409 Rome paid a large ransom to save itself. In 410, Alaric made a third try. The Romans refused to give him the land and power he demanded. So he marched his army into Rome, unconquered for almost 800 years.

Alaric, however, did not stay long in Rome. He still wanted land where his people could settle in peace. He led them south, planning to go on to Africa. But a storm destroyed their ships. They had to stop in southern Italy, where Alaric, their leader, died.

ALSO READ: ROME, ANCIENT.

ALASKA The name of the largest state in the United States comes from a word used long ago in the Aleutian Islands. These islands lie off the southwestern part of Alaska. Aleuts called the mainland *alakshak*, meaning a land bigger than the islands. And Alaska is a "great land"—over twice the size of the second largest state, Texas.

The Land Alaska can best be described in terms of three main parts.

TUNDRA. The cold, almost treeless plains called *tundra* lie along the western and northern coasts. In winter, the tundra is covered with ice and snow. Flowering plants and mosses appear when summer sunshine melts the ice. But ice underneath the surface does not melt, so the water does not drain off. The land is swampy all summer. The tundra slopes down to the Arctic Ocean north of Brooks Range mountains. Here the tundra is much colder in winter than it is on the west coast.

INTERIOR. The interior part of Alaska lies between two mountain ranges. On the north is Brooks Range. The Alaska Range is on the south. The interior stretches from the western tundra to the border of Can-

Although Alaska has very few people—only about one person to each square mile (2.6 sq. km)—its population has increased rapidly over the years. In 1940 the population of the state was 75,524; in 1960, 226,167; today there are half a million Alaskans.

▲ *An Eskimo woman busy making a hat for a hatmaking contest in Nanupitchuk, Alaska.*

Juneau, Alaska's capital since 1900, was settled in 1881 by gold miners and named for Joe Juneau, who made Alaska's first big gold discovery in 1880.

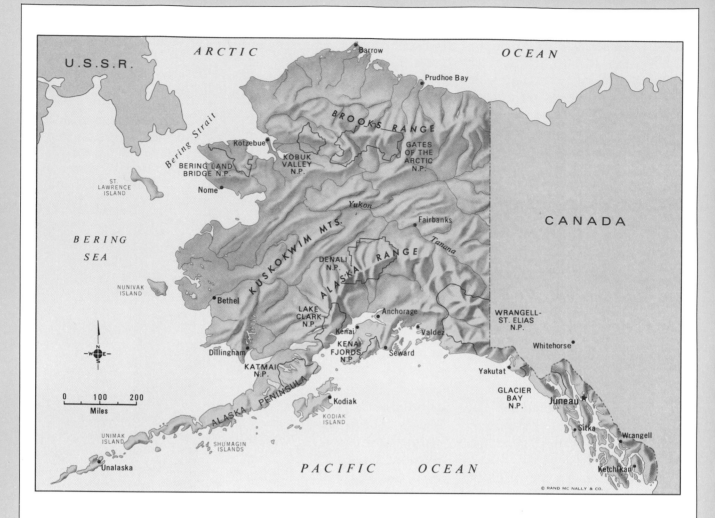

U.S.S.R.

ARCTIC   OCEAN

• Barrow

• Prudhoe Bay

Bering Strait

BROOKS RANGE

Kotzebue •

KOBUK VALLEY N.P.

GATES OF THE ARCTIC N.P.

BERING LAND BRIDGE N.P.

CANADA

ST. LAWRENCE ISLAND

Nome •

Yukon

• Fairbanks

Tanana

BERING SEA

KUSKOKWIM MTS.

DENALI N.P.

ALASKA RANGE

NUNIVAK ISLAND

Bethel •

LAKE CLARK N.P.

• Anchorage

WRANGELL- ST. ELIAS N.P.

Kenai •

• Valdez

• Whitehorse

N W E S

Dillingham •

KENAI FJORDS N.P.

• Seward

Yakutat •

KATMAI N.P.

ALASKA PENINSULA

GLACIER BAY N.P.

Juneau ★

0   100   200
Miles

• Kodiak

KODIAK ISLAND

• Sitka

• Wrangell

UNIMAK ISLAND

SHUMAGIN ISLANDS

PACIFIC   OCEAN

Ketchikan •

Unalaska •

© RAND MC NALLY & CO.

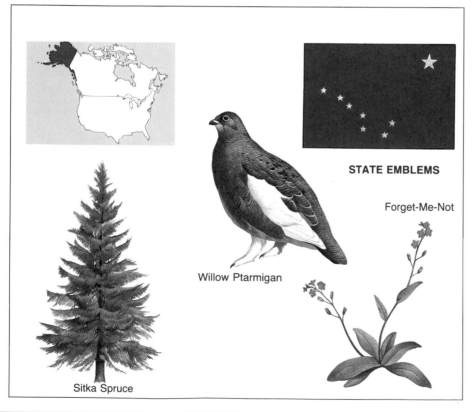

STATE EMBLEMS

Willow Ptarmigan

Forget-Me-Not

Sitka Spruce

ALASKA

Capital
Juneau (26,000 people)

Area
586,659 square miles
(1,518,659 sq. km) Rank: 1st

Population
521,000 people Rank: 49th

Statehood
January 3, 1959
(49th state admitted)

Principal river
Yukon River (1,265 miles/
2,036 km in Alaska)

Highest point
Mount McKinley 20,320
feet (6,193 m)

Largest city
Anchorage (227,000 people)

Motto
"North to the Future."

Song
"Alaska's Flag."

Famous people
Carl Eielson, Joe Juneau

ada. It is mostly the Yukon River basin.

Interior Alaska is colder in winter and warmer in summer than land nearer the ocean. Ocean temperature does not change so much as land temperature from summer to winter. Water is warmer than land in winter. It is cooler than land in summer. So winter winds from the ocean warm the land near the coast. And summer ocean winds cool the nearby land. Interior Alaska is not "protected" by the ocean, so its temperature changes much more from summer to winter.

SOUTH. Most of southern Alaska lies near the water. It follows the long southern coast. Southern Alaska may be divided into three sections.

The *southwest* consists of the Alaska Peninsula and many islands. Mount Katmai, a volcano, is near the northern end of the peninsula. This volcano has one of the largest craters in the world. The Valley of Ten Thousand Smokes was formed when Katmai erupted in 1912. Steam rises from thousands of holes that dot the valley floor.

At the eastern end of southern Alaska is the *panhandle*. This narrow strip has the Pacific Ocean on one side and the Coast Mountains on the other. Canada lies beyond the mountains. Green forests and blue water make the panhandle beautiful. It is a land of mild winters, cool summers, and much rain. The capital, Juneau, is in this region. A new state capital is under construction, at Willow.

Between the southwest and the panhandle is *south-central* Alaska. Winters are mild here, too. The Alaska Range keeps out icy winds from the north. And winds blowing over the warm Alaska Current in the ocean raise winter temperatures.

Summers are cool and short in south-central Alaska, but summer daylight is long. (Summer periods of daylight lengthen as you go north.) The extra hours of sunshine make northern crops grow fast. Huge cabbages, turnips, and potatoes grow in the Matanuska Valley. Over half of the crops raised in Alaska come from this one valley.

The People The population is small for such a large state. About one-sixth of the people are Eskimos, Indians, and Aleuts. Around 4 out of

Alaska is by far the largest state in the United States. It is more than twice the size of Texas, the second largest state. But Alaska has fewer people than any state. There is less than one person per square mile (2.6 sq. km).

87

▶ *A pipeline being built through the forest in Alaska to carry oil from the Arctic oil fields.*

▼ *Kodiak bears are very large brown bears of Alaska, and are found on Kodiak Island. These bears eat salmon from the cold rivers.*

every 10 Alaskans live in or near the city of Anchorage, which is by far the biggest city in the state.

History Alaska was the "front porch" of the Americas 30,000 years ago. At that time, there was probably a land or ice bridge connecting Asia and North America. The Bering Strait flows over it today. The first people to reach the New World crossed from Asia to Alaska. They were the ancestors of modern American Indians and Eskimos.

Most of the people moved southward. But some stayed in Alaska. When the first white men arrived in the early 1700's, the Tlingit and Haida Indians lived in the southeast, the Aleuts on the Alaska Peninsula and Aleutian Islands, and Eskimos in the far north and west. Russian fur traders from eastern Siberia sailed across the short Bering Strait to Alaska. They called the region *Russian America.*

The Russians came in search of furs. They fought the Eskimo and Indian hunters and killed a great many of them. Russia's czar (emperor) was in Moscow, half a world away. He found that he could not control his fur traders. Something else also worried him—Britain might capture Russian America. The land was too far away for the czar to defend.

He sold Russian America to the United States in 1867. The price was 7,200,000 dollars—less than 2 cents an acre! Alaska was truly a bargain. But many Americans did not think so at the time. They said that Secretary of State William H. Seward had wasted government money buying an "icebox." Many people called Alaska "Seward's Folly." They wondered how the huge northern land could be governed.

For the next 45 years, Alaska was neglected by the U.S. Government, which could not control the rough men who sailed there to get furs, fish, copper, and gold. Some U.S. companies built fish canneries in the 1890's. Alaska's gold rush from 1899 to 1902 brought thousands of prospectors and settlers to the Nome and Fairbanks regions. Finally, in 1912, Congress established Alaska as a U.S. territory, with criminal and civil laws. A U.S. farming colony was set up in the Matanuska Valley in the 1930's; the Alaska Highway was built in 1942. Alaska was declared a state in 1959.

Alaskans at Work This state differs from the other 49 in several ways. Because it is so far north, little farming is done. Nearly 97 percent of Alaska's land is owned by the United States Government. Many people who live in Alaska are members of the armed forces.

Manufacturing is the leading industry in Alaska. Food items, especially canned and frozen fish and crabs, head the list. Lumber and other wood products are second on the list of manufactured goods.

For many years, gold was Alaska's major mineral resource. However, with the discovery of oil on the Kenai Peninsula in 1957, large-scale drilling activity began throughout the state. In 1968, huge oil and natural gas reserves were found near Prudhoe Bay on Alaska's Arctic coast. The Alaska pipeline was built to carry the oil 800 miles (1,287 km) from the

Arctic region to the ice-free port of Valdez on the south coast. In 1977, oil began flowing through the pipeline.

Alaska's second most valuable resource is sand and gravel, which is used in highway construction. Coal, silver, platinum, and uranium are also mined. The state's mineral wealth has brought much economic growth and an influx of newcomers.

ALSO READ: ALEUT INDIANS; ARCTIC; ESKIMOS; INDIANS, AMERICAN.

ALBANIA North of Greece is Albania, the smallest Communist nation in Europe. Green valleys with many farming villages lie between rugged mountains. The larger towns can be reached by car. But pack animals are the only means of transportation to many mountain villages. In the mountains, the climate is moderate. But in summer it is hot on the beautiful sand beaches along the Adriatic Sea. (See the map with the article on EUROPE.)

Many women wear traditional baggy trousers and veils. Men often wear white felt caps, homespun breeches, and embroidered jackets. Albanians are known for their beautiful embroidery.

Foreign conquerors ruled Albania for many centuries. They came from the Italian peninsula, the Balkans, and the Middle East. Albania's na-

tional hero, Scanderbeg, fought fierce battles against the Turks in the fifteenth century. But the Turks conquered Albania in 1468 after Scanderbeg died. They made the country part of their territory, the Ottoman Empire. The Turks ruled Albania for more than 400 years. Most Albanians adopted the Turks' religion, Islam. Others were Orthodox Christians and Roman Catholics. Today, religion is banned by the Communist goverment.

In 1912 the Albanians finally overthrew the Turks and became independent. But Italian soldiers occupied Albania for four years during World War II. German troops later replaced the Italians. The Communist Party, led by Enver Hoxha, took over in

▲ *Most towns in Albania are small. Transportation is difficult in this mountainous land.*

ALBANIA

Capital City: Tirana (220,000 people).
Area: 11,100 square miles (28,748 sq. km).
Population: 3,000,000.
Government: Communist republic.
Natural Resources: Oil, natural gas, coal, water power.
Export Products: Oil, bitumen, chrome, copper, fruit, and vegetables.
Unit of Money: Lek.
Official Language: Albanian.

Alberta supplies about three-fourths of Canada's oil. It is known that there are enormous quantities of oil locked in the Athabasca tar sands in the northeast of the province. Experts believe that there could be as much oil in this one area as is known to exist in the rest of the world.

1946. Albania ended close relations with the U.S.S.R. in 1961 and was a loyal ally of China until 1978.

Albania is a poor country. Most Albanians are farmers. They raise tobacco, livestock, grain, fruits, and vegetables. Few own their land. Most farms are owned by the government. Albania is rich in mineral resources, notably oil, coal, copper, iron, and chromium, but they have not been fully developed. Enver Hoxha died in 1985, but Albania remained isolated from the outside world.

ALSO READ: COMMUNISM, EUROPE, OTTOMAN EMPIRE.

ALBATROSS   see SEABIRDS.

ALBERTA   Alberta is a western, or prairie, province of Canada. In both area (about the size of Texas) and population, it is the fourth largest of the ten Canadian provinces. Its principal cities are Edmonton (the capital), Calgary, Lethbridge, Red Deer, and Medicine Hat (named for the cap worn by an Indian medicine man). The province is named after a daughter of Queen Victoria.

The eastern side of Alberta has gently rolling prairie. The land builds up through foothills to the towering Rocky Mountains that form the province's border with British Columbia. Mt. Columbia, the highest of Alberta's peaks, is 12,294 feet (3,747 m) high. The southern part consists of

▶ *People who love nature would be happy here. This is part of Banff National Park in Alberta.*

treeless plains, and is one of the few sections of Canada with so little rainfall that it requires irrigation to keep its farmlands blooming. The central part is known as the *parklands*, because of its many small lakes, rivers, and forests. A feature of the province's winter climate is a warm wind called a *chinook*, which may change the temperature from 40°F below zero (−40°C) to 40°F (4°C) above in two hours. Alberta has more sunshine than any other Canadian province.

History   Some of the oldest traces of life in Canada are found in Alberta. The Drumheller Valley is famous as a dinosaur burial ground. Millions of years ago the region must have been a tropical jungle. Later, Alberta was covered by a polar ice cap. As the ice retreated, hardy Indian settlers arrived from Alaska. Their descendants, the Sarcee and Blackfoot tribes of the Athabascan-speaking and Algonkian-speaking families, still live in Alberta. Only 2 percent of Alberta's people are Indians. The rest are descendants of European immigrants. The first Europeans to arrive in the Canadian West were adventurers and fur traders from the Hudson's Bay Company of England. Today, about 45 percent of Alberta's people are of British origin or ancestry.

Alberta became part of the new Dominion of Canada in 1870. The Royal Canadian Mounted Police established outposts and forts, and the railway soon arrived from the East. Cattle ranching began. The land was ideal for growing a new type of wheat called *Marquis*. In 1905, Alberta became a province. It has a lieutenant-governor, like other Canadian provinces, an elected law-making assembly, and an executive council.

Industries   Coal, oil, and natural gas are found in Alberta in abundance. One-third of all Albertans earn their living from oil production and mining. Alberta's oil resources are vast: a

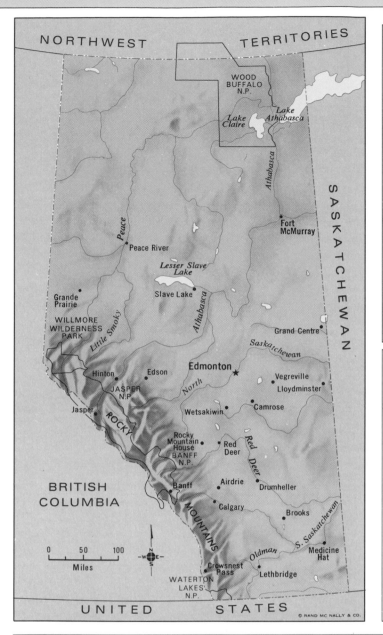

ALBERTA

Capital
Edmonton (687,000 people)

Area
255,285 square miles (661,137 sq. km)

Population
2,345,000 people

Entry into Confederation
September 1, 1905.

Principal river
Saskatchewan 1,205 miles (1,939 km)

Highest point
Mount Columbia 12,294 feet (3,811 m)

Largest city
Edmonton (6th largest Canadian city)

Famous People
Alexander Mackenzie, James Gladstone, Joe Clark

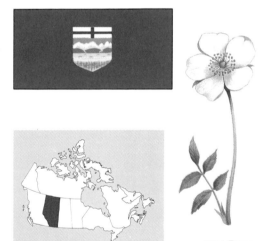

Wild Rose

◀ *The skyline of Calgary, one of Alberta's major cities. Notable landmarks are the Petro Canada Center and Calgary Tower.*

In some countries albino animals are sacred. White cattle are worshiped in India and white elephants in Thailand.

deposit near Lake Athabasca in the north is thought to contain the world's largest single reserve. Alberta petroleum is sent to much of Canada and the western United States. The province also has a large lumber industry.

Ranching and farming are important, though 7 out of 10 Albertans nowadays are town-dwellers. Alberta is Canada's major supplier of meat. Calgary is the cowboy capital of Canada, and every July plays host to the world's largest "stampede," or rodeo, with hundreds of contests of bronco-busting, steer-riding, and chuck-wagon races. Wheat and other grain crops are grown.

Many of the beautiful areas of Alberta have been set aside as national parks. One of the most popular is Banff National Park. Wood Buffalo Park in the north, at 17,300 square miles (44,800 sq. km), is the largest national park in the world. It is the home of the biggest herds of bison in North America, and is the nesting ground of the rare whooping cranes, which migrate to Alberta from southern Texas each year.

ALSO READ: CANADA, NATIONAL PARK.

ALBINO Animals, including human beings, are sometimes born with no coloring matter in their skin, hair, or eyes. They are albinos. White hair, pink eyes, and pinkish skin mark the albino.

Coloring matter in normal people and animals is called *pigment*. Pigments carry many colors: the yellow of a canary's wings, the stripes of zebras, the green of a cat's eyes. *Melanin*, a dark pigment, is the main coloring material of skin. A blonde person has less melanin than a black person. An albino's skin and eyes have no melanin. They look pink because blood vessels show through. Human albinos must wear dark glasses in the sun, because their eyes

have no pigment for protection from strong light. An albino's hair is snow white. Look at the squirrel in the photograph. Notice its eye color.

Not all albino animals are pure white. *Partial* albinos are more common. Most white horses, for example, have some coloring, perhaps blue eyes or a dark patch of skin. Certain black-and-yellow butterflies sometimes have white offspring, but with black markings on their wings. Rare white tigers have darkish stripes.

Albinos inherit their colorless condition from their ancestors, through *genes*, tiny parts of body cells. Genes control what a living thing inherits from its parents. An albino parent may produce normal young, and the young may later produce albinos. It may not happen again for many, many generations.

Plants can also produce albinos. They lack chlorophyll, a green material that makes food for the plant. Without food, albino plants quickly die.

ALSO READ: GENETICS, PHOTOSYNTHESIS, SKIN.

▲ *This albino (all-white) squirrel lacks the natural color of its relatives. Its eyes appear red from tiny blood vessels, normally masked by eye coloration.*

ALCHEMY From about the third century B.C. to the 1700's, the study of metals and elements was a strange blend of science, magic, and religion known as *alchemy*. It was the forerunner of the modern science of chemistry. Alchemy was practiced by the ancient Chinese, Egyptians, Greeks, and Romans. Greek alchemists first introduced the belief that all matter is a mixture of four basic elements—air, earth, fire, and water. They thought that every form of matter could be made by mixing these four elements in the right amounts. From the Greeks and Romans, the study of alchemy reached the Arabs, probably about the eighth century. Later in the Middle Ages it reached Europe.

The people who practiced alchemy had three main goals. First they

▲ *The German alchemist Hennig Brand discovered phosphorus in 1669. However, like all other alchemists, he failed in his attempt to change base metal into gold.*

wanted to change inexpensive common or "base" metals, such as lead, into gold, the "perfect" (and most valuable) metal. Second, they wanted to find a medicine that would cure all diseases. And third, they wanted to make a substance that would make old people young and allow them to live forever. Alchemists believed that there was a magical substance, called the *philosophers' stone*, that could do these three things. Many strange recipes were invented in an effort to make this "stone." Some alchemists cooked "witches' brews," using ingredients such as hairs, bats' wings, and spiders. Of course, these brews never succeeded in curing sick people. Nor did the alchemists ever find a way to make gold from other metals. But some of their experiments led to the discovery of new elements, such as phosphorus, used today to make matches and fertilizers. Alchemists also invented some useful medicines.

At the end of the 1700's, the practice of alchemy began to fade. People no longer believed that the philosophers' stone existed. They began to

see that many of the claims made by the alchemists were not based on scientific facts. But even though many of the alchemists' ideas were wrong, some of their discoveries helped pave the way for the development of modern chemistry.

ALSO READ: CHEMISTRY, ELEMENT, METAL, SCIENCE.

ALCOHOL   see DISTILLATION.

ALCOHOLIC BEVERAGE People probably made the first alcoholic beverage by accident, thousands of years ago. Someone might have kept some grape juice standing too long, before drinking it. When the person drank the juice, it probably tasted sour and made him feel dizzy.

What this person discovered was a chemical process called *fermentation*. Fermentation occurs when microorganisms, such as bacteria, yeast, and mold, are added to certain plant and animal substances. The two major products of fermentation are carbon dioxide, a gas, and alcohol, a colorless liquid. When the grape juice was left to stand too long, yeast spores fell into it from the air and grew in the juice. The juice fermented into an alcoholic beverage which has come to be called *wine*.

The manufacture of alcoholic beverages is one of the biggest industries today. Among the beverages made are beer, wine, whisky, gin, rum, and bourbon. Beer is made from cereal grains, and wine is made from fruits. Whisky is made from barley, gin is made from fermented grain flavored with juniper berries, and bourbon is made from corn. Fermented molasses produces rum.

Some people can drink alcoholic beverages in modest amounts without serious or long-lasting damage to their health. There are other people, however, who should never drink alcohol

Drunk driving is a crime. Organizations such as MADD (Mothers Against Drunk Drivers) and SADD (Students Against Driving Drunk) are helping to make motorists aware that they should never drink and drive.

▲ *Beer is a popular alcoholic beverage. Beer ferments in wooden vats as part of the brewing process.*

Edwin Aldrin had made a spaceflight before the historic 1969 moonlanding. In November, 1966 he partnered James A. Lovell aboard Gemini 12. During a 59-orbit mission, Aldrin spent over five hours working outside the spacecraft.

because they are victims of *alcoholism*, a serious health problem in the United States. There are about 10 million alcoholics in the U.S. Alcoholics are people who cannot stop themselves from drinking alcohol. They become *addicted* to alcohol.

Alcohol acts as a *depressant* on the body. A depressant dulls the centers of the brain that control speech, emotions, judgment, and coordination of movement. The depressant effects of alcohol become dangerous when a person drives an automobile after drinking alcoholic beverages. Alcohol may interfere with a driver's judgment, blur vision, and destroy muscle coordination. The U.S. National Highway Traffic Safety Administration has found that about two out of five drivers who are in car accidents that kill people have been drinking before driving.

Alcoholics Anonymous (A.A.) is an organization that has helped thousands of alcoholics conquer their addiction. A.A. helps alcoholics help one another solve their problems.

ALSO READ: ADDICTION, DISTILLATION, FERMENTATION, YEAST.

ALCOTT, LOUISA MAY (1832–1888)
Little Women, the story of a New England family during the Civil War, was written by Louisa May Alcott. She wrote the story about her own family. She was Jo, and her real-life sisters, May, Elizabeth, and Anna, were the other March sisters—Meg, Beth, and Amy.

Louisa May Alcott was born in Pennsylvania, but she lived most of her life in Massachusetts. "Orchard House" in Concord, Massachusetts, where she sometimes wrote, can be seen today. Ralph Waldo Emerson and Henry David Thoreau, famous writers, were the Alcotts' friends. They sometimes taught Louisa and her sisters.

Louisa's father, Amos Bronson Alcott, was a writer and teacher, too. He had ideas about education that most people of that time did not accept. For example, he believed girls should have a good education. He did not earn much. So Louisa tried all kinds of ways to earn money, including writing.

Louisa worked as a nurse during the Civil War. The letters she wrote about her experiences were made into a book and in 1869 she published *Little Women*, which was a great success. Money she earned from *Little Women* gave her a chance to spend time working in the women's suffrage movement (for voting) and in the temperance movement (against drinking alcoholic beverages).

Some of Louisa May Alcott's other well-loved books are *Little Men*, *Jo's Boys*, and *Under the Lilacs*.

ALSO READ: EMERSON, RALPH WALDO; THOREAU, HENRY DAVID.

ALDRIN, EDWIN (born 1930)
Astronaut Edwin "Buzz" Aldrin was the second person to walk on the moon. He was the pilot of *Eagle*, the Apollo 11 lunar module that carried Neil Armstrong and him to the surface of the moon on July 20, 1969. This was the first moonlanding.

Born in Glen Ridge, New Jersey, Aldrin is the only son of a United States Army officer. Aldrin graduated

▼ *Louisa May Alcott* (below, right) *wrote* Little Women. *It was the story of the four March sisters—Meg, Jo, Beth, and Amy* (below).

third in his class at West Point, the U.S. Military Academy. He joined the Air Force and became a jet pilot in the Korean War.

Buzz Aldrin studied space travel at the Massachusetts Institute of Technology, where he earned a doctor of science degree in astronautics. He became an expert in rendezvous and docking—the meeting and joining together of two craft moving through space. Aldrin's knowledge of rendezvous and docking techniques contributed to the success of the Apollo program.

Aldrin began astronaut training in 1964. His first space trip was in November 1966, on the Gemini 12 mission in Earth orbit, during which he worked in space outside his spacecraft for 5½ hours.

ALSO READ: ARMSTRONG, NEIL; ASTRONAUT; COLLINS, MICHAEL; MOON; SPACE TRAVEL.

ALEUT INDIANS The Aleutian Islands, off the Alaskan Coast, are the home of the Aleut Indians. The Aleuts call the islands the "birthplace of the winds" because strong, hurricane-like winds often blow there. Some Aleuts also live in the Pribilof Islands, other islands nearby, and the Alaskan peninsula.

For centuries, the hardy Aleuts relied for their living on the Pacific Ocean. Their boats, called *kayaks* and *umiaks*, were made of animal skins sewn together by Aleut women and stretched over a frame made of bone. There are no trees on the islands from which to make a wooden boat. The Aleuts used poison-tipped harpoons to kill seals, whales, and fish. They used seal oil and whale blubber as fuel. The Aleuts' homes were holes dug in the ground and covered with sod, driftwood, and whale bones.

The Aleuts are closely related to the Eskimos of Alaska. But the Aleuts spoke a language of their own, and had some different customs. The

Aleuts' ancestors wore long garments made of bird skin, with feathers turned to the inside for warmth. They also wore light raincoats with pointed hoods, made from strips of seal intestines and decorated with bird feathers. The Aleut women once sewed beautiful, colorful clothing, using tiny sewing needles made of bird bones.

About 30,000 Aleut Indians were living on the Aleutian Islands and the Alaskan mainland when Russian traders first arrived in 1741. Great numbers of the Aleuts were killed in massacres, or died from diseases, such as smallpox and tuberculosis, brought by the white people. Marriages between whites and Indians also reduced the number of full-blooded Aleuts. The old ways and customs of the Aleuts mostly vanished. Many of the Indians today have Russian names and are members of the Russian Orthodox Church. There are now only about 1,000 full-blooded Aleuts and about 5,500 of mixed blood.

ALSO READ: ALASKA; INDIANS, AMERICAN; ESKIMO.

▲ *Edwin "Buzz" Aldrin, the second astronaut to walk on the moon.*

▼ *Aleut women on Attu Island in the Pacific Ocean weave some of the finest baskets in the world.*

The empire of Alexander the Great.

▲ *Alexander the Great and his conquering armies brought a vast empire under Macedonian control. Egypt and Persia both fell to this brilliant general.*

When Alexander was a boy he tamed the great and spirited horse Bucephalus, a horse that no one else dared to ride. This famous horse carried Alexander as far as India, where it died. Alexander built a city and named it Bucephalo after his beloved steed.

ALEXANDER THE GREAT (356–323 B.C.) Alexander the Great was a mighty king and conqueror. He was one of the greatest military geniuses the world has ever known.

He was born in Pella, Macedonia. Alexander grew to be a handsome, brilliant man. Aristotle, the famous philosopher, came from Greece to teach him geography, politics, literature, medicine, and science. Alexander's father, King Philip II of Macedon, taught him to plan and win battles.

The young prince became king when he was 20. He then began the series of marches that continued until he ruled almost all of the then-known world. On his great war horse, Bucephalus, he first took over Greece. He went on to conquer southeastern Europe, Asia Minor, Egypt, and India. On his way he crushed the Persian Empire, and was made king of Egypt and Asia. He and his troops traveled over 11,000 miles (17,700

km). He spread Greek customs and ideas wherever he went.

In India his men refused to go farther. They were tired and frightened, and wanted to go home. Worn out, Alexander agreed to turn back. He died of fever in Babylon, at the early age of 33.

ALSO READ: ANCIENT CIVILIZATIONS, MACEDONIA.

ALFRED THE GREAT (849?–899) Alfred was the king of Wessex, the southernmost of four kingdoms that became England. He is remembered as "the Great" because he led his people, the West Saxons, against the Danes—who had invaded Wessex—and defeated them.

Alfred became king in 871, after his father and three brothers had all ruled and died. Alfred, as a prince, had helped fight off the invading Danes. As king, he led an army against them. The mightiest Danish invasion came in 877, when King Guthrum landed in Wessex with his army. Alfred lost a battle to Guthrum, and went into hiding. While in hiding, Alfred made new plans for battle, and he defeated the Danes in 878.

Alfred built ships and towers along the coast to fight off the Danish invaders, should they break the peace. The Danes did so, in 886. Alfred once again defeated them, and also took over London. He drove the Danes from southern England in 897.

Alfred believed in the importance of education. He helped translate several books from Latin into Anglo-Saxon (Old English). He asked teachers from Wales and the European continent to come to his kingdom to teach. He also set up a school, and encouraged the development of arts and industries.

ALSO READ: ANGLO-SAXONS, ENGLISH HISTORY, VIKINGS.

ALGAE The slimy green scum that often floats on shallow lakes or ponds is a kind of algae, the simplest of plants. *Algae* is the plural form of the word *alga*. The plural form is usually used. There are many kinds of algae. These plants grow on land in damp places as well as water. Sometimes they grow attached to rocks or stones along the shore or way out at sea and are called *seaweeds*. They grow on other plants, on wood, turtles, water fleas, and even within plants and animals. Much of the green stuff in an aquarium is algae.

Some algae are so small that a thousand of them will fit on the head of a pin. Others are large, stretching for hundreds of feet. Certain small, fresh- and salt-water algae, called *diatoms*, are single cells with "glassy" outer walls made of silica. Diatoms are found in plankton and are the major food of many water aminals.

Algae Groups All algae contain a pigment called *chlorophyll*, which gives plants their green color. But some algae contain other pigments that hide the green color. Although algae are plants, some of them can move about. They do this by sliding, twisting, gliding, or by floating with currents.

Most algae can be put in one of four groups according to their color—blue-green, green, brown, and red.

Blue-green algae, such as pond scum, are cells with no definite *nuclei* (cell centers). Cells of green algae have definite nuclei. Green algae grow in fresh and salt water, or in any place that is light, moist, and cool. Green algae make up the largest of the four main kinds of algae. *Kelp*, a seaweed, is a brown alga. Kelp is sometimes attached to rocks near the shore. Some forms of brown algae are so small that they can be seen only with a microscope. Others are more than 200 feet (61 m) long. Red algae can be found in oceans, especially in warm seas. Coral reefs are formed partly from red algae.

Useful Algae Algae are food for fish and other animals. Even humans use algae as food. A single tablespoon of the alga called *chlorella* has as much protein as an ounce of steak. Chlorella also contains vitamins, fats, and starches. As yet, it has not been made to taste good on its own, but it is a nourishing food.

The Japanese have made soup, noodles, tea, bread, and ice cream from kelp and other kinds of algae. The bread is pale green. So is the ice cream. But all these foods taste good. Algae are also used in food in the United States. Puddings thicken because of a product called *agar*, which comes from algae. You can also make algae cookies, using chlorella.

Why should people eat algae? For one thing, we may need new foods before very long. The number of people is growing faster than the food supply in many parts of the world. Science must find new foods. Some of these new foods may come from the plentiful supply of algae.

ALSO READ: CELL, FOOD WEB, PLANT, PLANT KINGDOM.

▲ *Alfred the Great, King of Wessex, led the English against the Danes.*

▼ *In the sea live many-celled algae called seaweeds. In fresh water are found pondweeds, such as* Spirogyra.

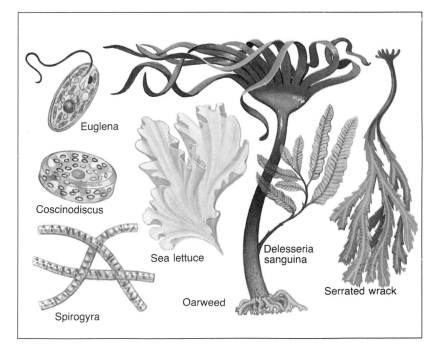

Euglena

Coscinodiscus

Spirogyra

Sea lettuce

Delesseria sanguina

Oarweed

Serrated wrack

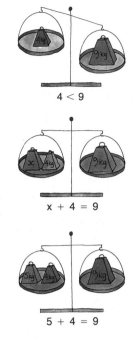

$4 < 9$

$x + 4 = 9$

$5 + 4 = 9$

▲ *An equation in algebra is like a balance scale. Four is less than nine. But if 9 kg are put on one pan and 4 kg plus 5 kg on the other, the scales will balance. In other words, $9 = 4 + 5$.*

▲ *Horatio Alger, Jr., wrote* the Ragged Dick *series which tell the stories of hardworking boys who lived a century ago. Alger's books about their adventures and success sold millions of copies.*

ALGEBRA Here are three math problems.

(1) What number would you add to 5 to get 7? $5 + \square = 7$.

(2) What number would you multiply by 3 to get 6? $\square \times 3 = 6$.

(3) What number would you subtract from 5 to get 3? $5 - \square = 3$.

In each of these examples, the correct number is 2. In (1), $5 + \boxed{2} = 7$; in (2), $\boxed{2} \times 3 = 6$; and in (3), $5 - \boxed{2} = 3$. Although you may not have known it, you were doing problems in algebra.

Several symbols, $+$, $\times$, $-$, $\square$, and $=$, are used in these problems. Symbols are a quick, easy way of getting across an idea. Algebra is a branch of mathematics which uses symbols.

Two of these symbols are very important. One is the symbol $=$. This symbol means "is equal to." It means that everything on the left of the symbol "is equal to" everything on the right of it. When the symbol $=$ is used, the group of symbols and numbers is called an *equation*.

The other important symbol is $\square$. When you first considered the problem, you did not know what number went in the box. The correct number was *unknown* to you. The symbol $\square$ in the examples is called an *unknown* for this reason. The problem was to find the *unknown number*. The symbol for an unknown is not usually a box. It is usually a letter, such as x, t, or v. Problem (1) written with a letter instead of a box would look like this:

$$5 + x = 7.$$

The mathematician knows that x stands for an unknown number. To solve the problem, you have to find a number to use for x that will make the equation true. So algebra can also be the study of rules that help you find an unknown number.

■ **LEARN BY DOING**

How Algebra Is Used Here is an example of how algebra can be used to help you solve mathematical prob-lems. Suppose you are an athlete, planning a training session. You plan to run for 30 minutes. You can run one lap of the running track in 5 minutes. If you keep up the same speed, how many laps will you run in in your training session?

The unknown number is x (the number of laps). The equation to work it out is $x = 30 \div 5$: the number of laps (x) is equal to the total running time (30 minutes) divided by your time for each lap (5 minutes). How many laps will you run in the planned training sesson? ■

This is a simple example, but algebra problems can be more difficult. Scientists often use algebraic equations in their work. The unknown might be how much fuel to put in a rocket, or how many seeds to plant in a cornfield.

History of Algebra One of the oldest pieces of writing ever found is about algebra. The writing was carved on stone thousands of years ago by an Egyptian named Ahmes. The equation written on the stone is $\frac{x}{7} + x = 19$.

It took a long time for the study of algebra to progress. Greeks, Indians, Persians, and others knew a little about algebra. The Arabs learned more about algebra than any other people. An Arab mathematician wrote a book in 825, called *Hisab al-jabr w' almuqabalah*, meaning "the science of equations." We get our word "algebra" from the *al-jabr w'* in the title. The Persian poet Omar Khayyam wrote a book on algebra in the late 11th century.

A Frenchman, François Vieta (1540–1603), is known as the "father of modern algebra." He collected all the known writings on algebra, and added many new ways to prove that algebraic equations are true. Since Vieta's time, algebra has grown and changed. Mathematicians today use many different kinds of algebra to solve many different kinds of problems.

ALSO READ: ARITHMETIC, MATHEMATICS, NUMBER.

ALGER, HORATIO, JR. (1832–1899)

"Poor but honest boy works hard to win fame and fortune." This "rags-to-riches" idea made Horatio Alger, Jr., one of America's most popular writers of novels in the 1800's.

Alger was born in Revere, Massachusetts. His family expected him to follow in his father's footsteps as a Unitarian minister. But he had plans of his own. After graduation from Harvard, Horatio traveled, and then worked as a private teacher and as a newspaperman. He returned to Massachusetts after several years, and gave in to his family's wishes. He became a Unitarian minister in 1864. Two years later, he moved to New York City and became the chaplain of the Newsboys' Lodging House, a home for orphans and runaway boys. The ideas for the stories that later made Alger famous came from the young people at the home. His first successful book was *Ragged Dick*, published in 1867. His stories showed that anyone could make good if he or she tried hard enough.

ALSO READ: CHILDREN'S LITERATURE.

◀ *Ancient Roman buildings are part of the historic heritage of Algeria.*

ALGERIA The African nation of Algeria covers a very large area. It is the second largest country in Africa—only Sudan has a larger area—and is one-fourth the size of the United States. It is bordered by seven other countries and the Mediterranean Sea. The Sahara Desert covers most of Algeria. Few people live in the vast region of rocky plains and great sand dunes, where rain may not fall for years. There are valuable mineral resources beneath the desert. (See the map with the article on AFRICA.)

The people of the Sahara are nomads, wandering from oasis to oasis, caring for their goats and camels and living in animal-skin tents. But most Algerians are crowded into the more fertile narrow strip of land along the Mediterranean Sea. Algiers is the

In Algeria, 47 percent of the population is under 15 years of age. Four percent is over 65. About 25 percent of Algerians can read and write.

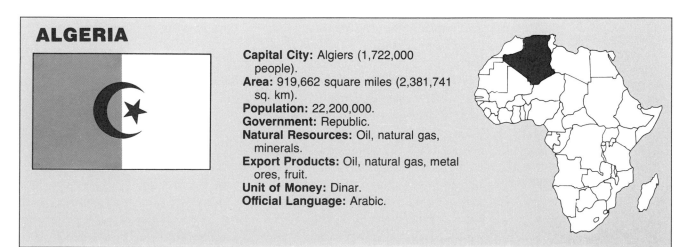

ALGERIA

Capital City: Algiers (1,722,000 people).
Area: 919,662 square miles (2,381,741 sq. km).
Population: 22,200,000.
Government: Republic.
Natural Resources: Oil, natural gas, minerals.
Export Products: Oil, natural gas, metal ores, fruit.
Unit of Money: Dinar.
Official Language: Arabic.

▲ *A warrior, dressed in eagle feather warbonnet, of the Blackfeet, an Algonkian-speaking tribe of Great Plains Indians.*

Ethan Allen, one of the Green Mountain Boys in the American Revolution, told the Continental Congress that he was fighting for the independence of Vermont, not for the United States. Vermont declared its independence in 1779, but the Congress refused to let the state go. Ethan Allen then told the British that he wanted the state to be made a part of Canada. This was also refused.

largest city and port, and the nation's capital.

The first known settlers of the region were the ancient Berbers. However, Arabs conquered the land about a thousand years ago, and most Algerians are now Arabo-Berbers, who speak Arabic and follow the religion of Islam. A few Algerian Berbers still cling to their old language and customs.

Many nations have controlled Algeria. It was called Numidia under ancient Roman rule. Arabs seized the country later on, then the Turks in the 1500's. The French captured Algeria in 1830, to stop pirates who hid there. The French stayed and slowly gained control of the whole country. The Algerians grew unhappy with French control, especially after World War II. They began to rebel in 1954. The Algerians and the French fought for eight years and more than 250,000 people died before Algeria won independence in 1962.

Algeria is now a republic. Beneath its desert sands lies oil, and this provides much of the country's wealth. Algeria also has reserves of natural gas and other minerals. Social and economic reforms are bringing great changes to the lives of the Algerian people.

ALSO READ: AFRICA, BARBARY COAST, SAHARA DESERT.

ALGONKIAN Algonkian is a family of languages used by a large number of North American Indian tribes. The name is also spelled *Algonquian*. Algonkian-speaking Indians moved from Alaska to eastern Canada and the northern United States sometime before 3000 B.C. Each tribe adapted to its new surroundings. Tribes in Canada and New England hunted deer and moose, wore buckskins, and lived in bark-covered tepees or wigwams. New England tribes also learned to tap the sweet sap from

sugar maple trees. Those in marshy regions near the Great Lakes gathered wild rice.

Algonkian-speaking people along the eastern seaboard met the first white settlers who sailed ships from Europe to the New World. The Indians taught the colonists how to plant corn, pumpkins, and squash; bake clams; make canoes; use seaweed for fertilizer, and even how to smoke tobacco. Without the Indians' help, the colonists would not have survived.

Algonkian-speaking tribes in the northeast included the Delaware, Menominee, Illinois, Narraganset, Mahican, and Powhatan. Other Algonkian-speaking Indians lived in the Great Plains. They included the Arapaho, Blackfoot, and Cheyenne. The Naskapi, Cree, Ojibwa, Montagnais, and Algonkin tribes roamed eastern Canada. The Algonkin tribe, which gave its name to this language family, lived along the Ottawa River. They are now often called Ottawa Indians.

You may not realize it, but you already know some Algonkian words. The English colonists borrowed *racoon*, *pecan*, and *squash* from Algonkian-speaking Indians, for example. Many American place names come from Algonkian words, too. Examples are Manhattan, Chicago, Illinois, Massachusetts, Mississippi, and Wisconsin.

ALSO READ: INDIANS, AMERICAN.

ALIMENTARY CANAL see DIGESTION.

ALLEN, ETHAN (1738–1789) Ethan Allen was a hero of the American Revolution. He was born on a Connecticut farm, and planned to enter Yale College. But his father died when Ethan was 16. He had to go to work to support his family.

▲ *Ethan Allen, a hero of the American Revolution, demanding the surrender of Fort Ticonderoga at the start of the Revolutionary War.*

He served with the citizens' army (militia) during the French and Indian War (1754–1763). He moved to what is now Vermont when he was 31. He later helped to form the Green Mountain Boys, and he became their leader. These brave frontiersmen defended their farms from New Yorkers, who considered the region part of New York. When the Revolutionary War began in 1775, Allen and Colonel Benedict Arnold led the Green Mountain Boys in the daring capture of Fort Ticonderoga from the British. Allen joined a small group who tried to seize Montreal later that year. He was captured by the British and spent nearly three years in jail in England. After his release in 1778, he wrote the hair-raising autobiography, *Narrative of Colonel Ethan Allen's Captivity.*

Allen tried to convince Congress to make Vermont a state after the Revolution. But not until two years after his death in 1789 was Vermont admitted to the Union.

ALSO READ: AMERICAN REVOLUTION, VERMONT.

ALLERGY You probably have an allergy, if playing with a dog seems to make you sneeze, or if you feel itchy after eating chocolate. You are "sensitive" to something—your body does not like it.

The human body has a built-in safety device that sets off an alarm signal in the bloodstream if something harmful, such as a germ, enters the body. When it gets the signal, the blood begins to release disease-fighting substances called *antibodies.* In some people, the alarm signal goes off in response to something that to others is not harmful at all—such as dog hairs or chocolate. When this happens, antibodies increase the production of substances called *histamines,* which cause an allergic reaction, such as sneezing, itching, or vomiting.

A substance to which a person is allergic is called an *allergen.* It might be something a person swallows, breathes in, or touches. One of the most common allergies is *hay fever,* which is caused by pollen in the air.

Once a doctor has discovered what the allergen is, the doctor may tell the patient to avoid exposure to it, or he may give him a drug called an *antihistamine.* This drug counteracts the histamines in the body and thus stops the allergic reaction. Antihistamines were discovered by a Swiss chemist, Daniel Bovet, who received the Nobel Prize in 1957 for his work.

A doctor can also treat an allergy by giving the patient injections (shots). These shots contain tiny amounts of the allergen itself—so tiny that the body does not react. Then, over a period of time, increasing amounts of the allergen are injected. The body gets used to the allergen and no longer reacts when coming in contact with it.

Doctors can treat, and sometimes cure, allergies, although they still do not understand everything about them. Much remains to be learned about why some people have them, while others do not.

ALSO READ: ANTIGEN AND ANTIBODY, BLOOD, DISEASE.

About one person in seven in the United States has an allergy that needs medical attention. Allergies tend to run in families. If both parents have an allergy, each of their children has about a 75 percent chance of developing one.

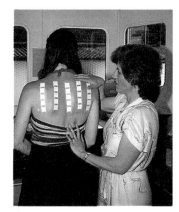

▲ *Sometimes a person shows an allergic reaction, but does not know what has caused it. To find out, doctors may test different allergens on the patient's skin.*

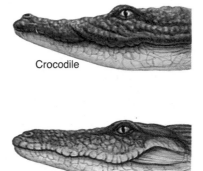

Crocodile

Alligator

▲ *One way to tell a crocodile from an alligator: when a crocodile closes its jaws, the fourth tooth of the lower jaw can still be seen. In alligators and their relatives, the tooth fits into a hole in the upper jaw and cannot be seen.*

ALLIGATORS AND CROCODILES Biologists believe that alligators and crocodiles have lived in rivers and swamps in many of the warm parts of the world for about 135 million years. They are found today in Asia, Africa, Australia, and North and South America.

Alike but Different Alligators and crocodiles look alike in many ways. But there are differences, apart from their different names. Ancient Romans saw one of these animals basking in the North African sun and called it *crocodilus*, meaning "worm of the pebbles." The English word "crocodile" came from this name. Spaniards saw a similar reptile in the New World and called it *el lagarto*, meaning "the lizard." From this, came the word "alligator."

Crocodiles generally grow to be longer than alligators, although both start out life as tiny babies—a few inches long—hatched from eggs. Crocodiles 30 feet (9 m) long have been seen, but alligators are rarely longer than 15 feet (4.5 m). Crocodiles are found in both fresh and salt water, while alligators prefer fresh water. Crocodiles have more green in their body color than alligators do.

In spite of their differences, alliga-

tors and crocodiles both belong to the same order of reptiles, *Crocodylia*. Members of this order are called *crocodilians*. Other crocodilians are the gavial of southern Asia, a close relative of the crocodile, and the long-snouted caiman, a Latin American cousin of the alligator.

Crocodilians have a tough, leathery skin covering an armor of bony plates. Temperature is very important to a crocodilian because, like all reptiles, it is a cold-blooded animal. It dies if its body becomes too hot or too cold. So it usually crawls up from its mudbank in the morning, basks in the warm sun until its body temperature rises.

On land, the crocodilian walks with its body high off the ground, dragging its long, powerful tail. Its rear legs are longer than its front ones. In the water, the animal swims by swishing its tail from side to side. The tail is also used as a weapon, for defense.

A crocodilian is well suited for a life spent hunting in the water. Its eyes and nostrils are on top of its head, so it can see and breathe when the rest of its body lies hidden underwater. It closes its nostrils to seal off its nose when it dives.

Crocodilians prey on birds, fish, and small mammals. The largest crocodilians are strong enough to drag

▶ *The American crocodile lives in salt water. It is darker and greener than the alligator. The American crocodile is rare.*

a cow or a horse into the water, and some kinds of crocodilians will attack people. Sharp teeth grip and hold the prey. New teeth grow in if some rip out. One animal was reported to have grown 45 sets of teeth by the time it grew to 13 feet (4 m) in length. Crocodilian teeth are sharp, but they are not strong enough to chew prey. The animal swallows its prey whole or tears it up by twisting it into pieces. The muscles that close the jaws are extremely strong, allowing the crocodilian to snap its mouth shut quickly. The muscles that open the jaws are weaker.

The Alligators There are two species of alligators, the *Chinese alligator* found in the Yangtze River and the larger *American alligator*. The American alligator lives in the southern United States, mostly in swamps in Louisiana, Georgia, South Carolina, and the Everglades of Florida.

Crocodilians, notably alligators, make a wide variety of sounds, from grunts and hisses to roars that can be heard a mile away. Alligators were once common, but so many were killed for their hides or for sport that they became scarce and were listed as an endangered species. But alligators have now increased so rapidly in Florida and other coastal areas that limited hunting of them is permitted.

Food for an alligator can be anything that it can outswim, ambush, or overpower. In the stomach of one dead alligator, a zoologist found several pieces of wood, a fishing sinker, and a crumpled can. The alligator had swallowed these objects to help grind the coarse food it could not chew.

Like other reptiles, crocodilians lay eggs. Most female crocodilians bury their eggs in sand or in a pile of leaves. The American alligator, however, builds a mound of plants up to 4 feet (1.2 m) high. The female lays from 30 to 70 hard-shelled eggs that hatch in nine weeks. The mother remains near the nest to guard the eggs. After the

eggs hatch, she helps her young find their way out of the nest to begin life in the water. Most of the young alligators stay with their mother until the next spring.

In Central and South America live relatives of the alligators, the caimans, also called *jacares*. The *black caiman* is the largest, reaching a length of 12 feet (3.7 m). The smallest is the *dwarf caiman*, rarely more than 4 feet (1.2 m) long.

The Crocodiles Some American crocodiles share southern Florida swamps with the American alligator. But the crocodile is quite rare in the U.S. Most American crocodiles live in South America.

The *American crocodile* is up to 14 feet (4.3 m) long. Like the American alligator, it eats fish and small animals. It will attack a person only in self-defense. The most dangerous crocodile is the *Nile crocodile*. It lives in African rivers and lakes, and was regarded as sacred in ancient Egypt. The *estuarine crocodile* is found mostly in coastal swamps and in the mouths, or estuaries, of large rivers, but often swims to sea. This habit probably explains why the species is found over such a wide range—from India southward to northern Australia. Both Nile and estuarine crocodiles can be 20 feet (6 m) long.

The smaller *marsh crocodile*, or *mugger*, is found in India and Sri Lanka. The *gavial* of northern India has a very slender snout that looks like the handle of a frying pan. The gavial may grow up to 20 feet (6 m) in length. It feeds mainly on fish that it catches by snaps of its long jaws.

ALSO READ: DINOSAUR, LIZARD, REPTILE.

▲ *In the United States alligators were once hunted for their hides. A bigger threat to them now is water pollution.*

An alligator can break a person's arm with one snap of its jaws. But the muscles that *open* the creature's jaws are so weak that a man can hold the alligator's mouth shut with only one hand.

▲ *This strange face was made in bronze in prehistoric times. Bronze was probably the first alloy made.*

ALLOY You might think that a bright new penny is copper. But a penny is not all copper. It is an alloy of copper, tin, and zinc. A mixture of two or more metals, or a metal and a non-metallic element, is an alloy.

Fewer than 80 pure metals exist naturally, but thousands of alloys can be made from them. The first alloy was *bronze*, which was made as long ago as 3000 B.C. Bronze was probably first discovered by accident, when copper and tin melted together and hardened. Alloys are still usually made by heating the metals until they melt and turn into liquids. The liquids are then mixed and allowed to cool. The solid that forms after cooling is the alloy.

Alloys are used for many purposes. They are used most often to make objects less expensive or more useful than objects composed of pure metals. Pure gold is beautiful, but a ring of pure gold bends and scratches easily. A ring of less expensive gold alloy is much stronger. A reddish-yellow ring is probably made of an alloy of gold and copper. A white or silvery gold ring may be an alloy of gold and nickel, called *white gold*.

Steel is one of the most useful alloys made today. It is a mixture of iron and other metals or non-metals, such as carbon and manganese. Other substances can be added to make the exact kinds of steel needed for special purposes. One example is the special steel alloy used to make steel sinks.

Pure steel would rust very quickly, so an alloy of steel, chromium, and nickel is used. Rust cannot form easily on a *stainless* steel sink. A smooth ride in a car is possible because of the springs between the passengers and the wheels. The springs would break if they were not very strong. An alloy of steel and vanadium makes them strong. Other parts of a car are also made of steel and other alloys.

Many different alloys of steel are used in building large buildings and ships. As metal scientists, or *metallurgists*, learn more about metals, they are developing many other alloys that can do some jobs better than steel. One example is carboloy—an alloy of carbon, cobalt, and tungsten—that is used to make cutting tools.

Alloys are very important in building airplanes. A plane made of pure steel would be very strong, but it would be so heavy that it would need immensely powerful engines. Aluminum is a very light metal, but an airplane of pure aluminum would not be strong enough. An alloy of aluminum, copper, manganese, and magnesium is often used to build airplanes, because it is both strong and light. This alloy was discovered by a German metallurgist in 1910. Alloys are also very important in building high-speed jets, missiles, and space rockets. Such craft must be able to resist heat, cold, and the stresses of supersonic flight.

ALSO READ: IRON AND STEEL, METAL.

▼ *The metals that go into a stainless steel fork.*

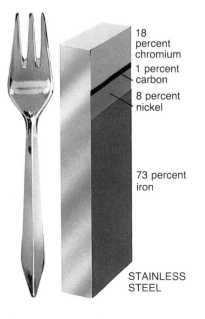

18 percent chromium
1 percent carbon
8 percent nickel

73 percent iron

STAINLESS STEEL

SOME COMMON OBJECTS AND THEIR ALLOY MAKE-UP	
Object	Metals in alloy (Metal shown first has largest amount in object)
Brass door knob	Copper and zinc
Aluminum pots and pans	Aluminum, copper, and manganese
Dime	Copper and nickel
14-carat yellow gold ring	Gold and copper
Stainless steel knives and forks	Stainless steel, which is made up of steel (iron and carbon), chromium, and nickel.

ALMANAC An almanac is a book full of all kinds of useful information. Most almanacs have a calendar and facts about countries, governments, history, and geography. They may also have weather information for cities and countries all over the world, and tables that tell the movements of the sun, planets, and stars.

People have written almanacs for thousands of years. The first ones, made in ancient Persia, contained astrologers' predictions. The word "almanac" probably comes from the Arabic *almanakh*, for "calendar." One of the most famous American almanacs was *Poor Richard's Almanac*, written by Benjamin Franklin. The book contained poetry, proverbs, astronomy, and weather information. Today most almanacs, such as *The World Almanac*, *The U.S. Fact Book*, and *The Statesman's Year Book*, contain general information and tell the reader about events that happened during the past year. Some organizations, such as the United Nations, publish special almanacs that give facts about many countries. Farmers and sailors still use almanacs to tell when the sun will rise and set or tides will rise and fall.

■ **LEARN BY DOING**

You might enjoy making your own almanac, based on events at home or at school. You could predict when the first snow will fall, or when you will go on vacation. Other entries might show game scores of your favorite team; birthdays of family, friends, and pets; or notes on books, movies, and hobbies. ■

ALSO READ: ASTROLOGY; FRANKLIN, BENJAMIN; REFERENCE BOOKS.

ALPHABET All written languages are made up of marks called *symbols*. In most languages today, these symbols are *letters* that stand for the sounds of the language. An alphabet is a list of these letter symbols, arranged in a particular order. The word "alphabet" comes from *alpha* and *beta*, the first two symbols, or letters, of the Greek alphabet. Our English alphabet of 26 letters is sometimes known as the ABC's.

Humans first tried to write down language when they made pictures of objects by scratching or painting them on surfaces. Some of these pictures told a story or gave a message. For instance, simple pictures of a person, a boat, and the sun rising in the sky might have meant, "I will make a trip down the river tomorrow morning."

People later began to use pictures to stand for words rather than for stories or ideas. Little by little, these pictures became simple shapes or marks that symbolized the separate *syllables* of words.

The earliest alphabets were probably developed sometime before 1000 B.C. The Phoenicians, who lived in the fertile regions east of the Mediterranean Sea, used an alphabet that may have come from earlier Egyptian *hieroglyphics*, a system of picture writing. But the symbols of the Phoenician alphabet were not picture ideas. The symbols became letters, each of which stood for a separate *consonant* sound of language. It was the first real alphabet.

The Phoenicians were great sailors and traders and they carried their alphabet on westward voyages to Europe and Africa. Other peoples wrote their own alphabets, using the Phoenicians' idea of setting symbols down in regular order, naming them, and having each one represent certain sounds. But the Phoenicians' alphabet had no *vowels*. Can you figure out this line from a well-known nursery rhyme written without vowels?

TH CW JMPD VR TH MN

The Greeks used the Phoenician letters, but made many changes.

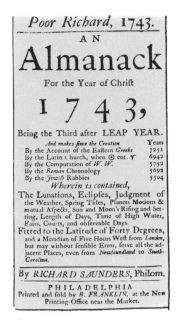

▲ *The title page of* Poor Richard's Almanac, *published by Benjamin Franklin. Some people read this almanac for its funny stories. Others wanted to find out things about the future.*

Did you know that the 26 letters of our alphabet can be arranged in 620,448,401,733,239,439, 369,000 different ways?

The oldest letter in our alphabet is O. It has remained the same since it was first used by the Phoenicians over 3,000 years ago. The newest letters in the English alphabet are V and J. They were not in use in Shakespeare's time, the late 1500's.

PHOENICIAN	ANCIENT GREEK	MODERN ENGLISH
K ∤	A	A
9 9	B	B
⅂	Γ	C G
△ ⅃	Δ	D
∃ ∃	E	E
Y	F	F
⊏ ⊏	Z	Z
⅄	H	H
⊗	Θ	
⫫	I	I J
Ψ Y	K	K
ϭ L	Λ	L
ϻ ϻ	M	M
Y	N	N
∓ Ξ Ξ	Ξ	X
O	O	O
⌐ ⌐	Π	P
⫯ ⫯	Ϙ	Q
ϞϞϞ	Ρ	R
⅂	Σ	S
w	T	T
X	Υ	U V
	Φ	W
	X	
	Ψ	Y
	Ω	

▲ *The first alphabet, with letters standing for sounds, was the Phoenician alphabet. You can see that modern English and ancient Greek alphabets have some letters in common.*

▼ *Letters from the Etruscan alphabet. Etruria was an ancient kingdom in Italy.*

They were the first to develop an alphabet with vowel sounds. With these new vowel letters, one could write the nursery rhyme line as,

THE COW JUMPED OVER THE MOON

This Greek practice was later copied by Etruscans, whose alphabet was in turn copied by the Romans. The Romans created their own symbols. A modern form of the Roman, or *Latin*, alphabet is now used most often in the Western world. Our own ABC's are Roman letters. Roman letters are also used for some of the languages of Africa, which did not have written forms of their own.

Early alphabets had only *capital*, or *upper-case*, letters. Later, to save space, small, or *lower-case*, letters were made. Being more rounded, these letters were easier to write, too.

Several other alphabets are used in the world today besides the modernized Latin symbols. Greeks still use the Greek alphabet. But modern Greek uses sounds and rules for writing and speaking different from those in ancient times. Russians and other Slavic peoples use the *Cyrillic* alphabet, based on old Greek. The alphabets of modern *Hebrew* and modern *Arabic* developed from Aramaic, a language spoken and written in Palestine during the time of Christ. Modern Hebrew is spoken today in Israel. *Early Hebrew*, a much older language, was used to write the Old Testament of the Bible.

Chinese is the only major language of the modern world whose writing is not alphabetical. Its symbols, known as *characters*, stand for words instead of sounds. However, in modern China, a uniform written language based on sounds, is being developed. Japanese writing is based on old Chinese characters, but some symbols represent syllables instead of words.

Without a written alphabet, you could never read a book, or write a letter to a friend, or use a computer. And when your mother sent you to the store, you would have to remember everything very carefully, because you could not make a list!

■ LEARN BY DOING

You can have fun by making up your own alphabet to stand for the sounds of the English language. You can start anywhere and make up your own order. What will you do with the sound "a"? Will your letter be long and pointed like an arrow, or rounded like an acorn? Or will you just make a funny little squiggle? What about the "b" sound? Could this look like a ball or a boat, or will it just be one special shape that always means "b"?

Write down, then say, the words "car," and "kite." Does your alphabet need two different letters for these sounds ("c" and "k")? Can you use one letter for both? What will you do when "c" sounds like "s," as in "cereal"? Would one letter be enough there? What about the "a" sounds in "father" and "face"? Some alphabets use one letter for each sound of the language. Other alphabets use one letter for more than one sound. Will your alphabet use one letter or two to show the "a" sounds of "father" and "face"? Think of other sounds for

which you might want separate letters. How many letters will your alphabet use? ■

ALSO READ: ARABIC, BRAILLE, CHINESE, HIEROGLYPHICS, WRITTEN LANGUAGE.

ALPS MOUNTAINS The Alps form the largest mountain system in Europe. They curve for 700 miles (1,127 km) from the French Riviera coast, along the French-Italian border, through Switzerland and Austria, and into Yugoslavia. Mont Blanc, 15,771 feet (4,807 m) high, is the highest peak in France and the highest in the Alps. (See the map with the article on EUROPE.)

Have you read the book *Heidi* by Johanna Spyri? Heidi lived in Switzerland with her grandfather and his goats in a high pasture called an *alp*. This Swiss word gave the mountains their name. Many of the people in the Alps today still live in villages in the meadows between peaks. Farmers herd cows and goats high in the mountains in summer, bringing the animals down to shelter in winter. Skilled craftsmen make watches, clocks, toys, and wood carvings.

Mountaineers come to challenge the rocky peaks of the Alps. Snow collects on the mountain slopes, and every winter thousands of people flock to the Alps to ski and enjoy other winter sports. Tourists are also attracted year-round to the lovely scenery of the Alps. Waterfalls pour hundreds of feet down the sides of the mountains. Melted snow flows into deep, blue lakes and into large rivers such as the Danube, Rhine, Rhône, and the Po. Roads and railroads pass beneath the Alps through tunnels, such as the Simplon. Other roads wind over passes, such as the Brenner and Simplon passes.

ALSO READ: EUROPE, GLACIER, MOUNTAIN, SWITZERLAND.

▲ *The Alps have many high mountains including Mont Blanc, the Matterhorn and the Jungfrau.*

AMAZON Greek myths told of a group of fierce women warriors called Amazons. The myths say that these warlike women lived near the Black Sea in Asia Minor, in what is now Turkey. Theirs was a land ruled by women. When the Amazons captured a man, they made him a slave. They taught their girl children to hunt and fight. They sent away their boy babies. The Amazons were ruled by Queen Hippolyta.

Hercules, a hero of Greek mythology, ventured among the Amazons to take Hippolyta's girdle, or belt. She gave it to him, but they argued, and Hercules killed Hippolyta.

ALSO READ: HERCULES, MYTHOLOGY.

▼ *According to legend, Amazons were a race of warrior women who were ruled by a queen and raised only girl children. They fought the Greeks during the Trojan War.*

▶ *The Amazon River winds through thick forest on its way to the Atlantic Ocean. A small number of Amazonian Indians still live by hunting fish with spears.*

The Amazon pours out so much fresh water into the Atlantic Ocean that more than 100 miles (160 km) out at sea from the great river's mouth the ocean's water is still fresh. The Amazon is so wide that the water pouring from its mouth is one-fifth of all the moving fresh water on Earth.

▼ *This fly was trapped in resin millions of years ago when the resin fossilized. The fly was preserved in amber.*

sloths, many kinds of insects, and many interesting plants. The flesh-eating piranha fish live in the river. Until the settlers came, the Amazon forest was home to scattered Indian tribes. Few Indians now follow their old way of life, as the modern world has brought change and industry to the Amazon basin.

ALSO READ: AMAZON; BRAZIL; INDIANS, AMERICAN; JUNGLE; RIVER; SOUTH AMERICA.

AMAZON RIVER The Amazon River and its tributaries (smaller rivers) make up the largest river system in the world. The Amazon begins high in the Andes Mountains and empties into the Atlantic Ocean, almost 4,000 miles (6,440 km) away. As the Amazon flows east across most of northern Brazil, it is fed by rivers from Peru, Venezuela, Colombia, Ecuador, and Bolivia. (See the map with the article on SOUTH AMERICA.) Only the Nile, in Africa, of all the rivers in the world, is longer than the Amazon. But the Amazon carries more water than any other river.

Francisco de Orellana, a Spaniard, first explored the Amazon in 1541. He later told how he and his men battled with female warriors. He gave the river its name because he thought they were the Amazons, the famous fighting women of Greek mythology.

Regular steamship service up the Amazon began in the 19th century, and settlements developed along the river banks. Today, even though new roads have opened up the country, and people have moved in to settle the land, much of the Amazon region remains unexplored. Most of the Amazon basin (land drained by the river) is a vast, dense jungle—the largest and most valuable rain forest in the world. The basin is about three-fourths the size of the United States. It is the home of animals, such as alligators, anacondas, monkeys, and

AMBASSADOR see FOREIGN SERVICE.

AMBER A piece of amber looks very much like a stone, but it is actually a fossil substance that formed from the sticky, gummy resin of pine trees millions of years ago. The resin was buried, and it hardened after many years in the ground.

Amber is usually golden or reddish-brown. It is almost transparent. In some pieces you can see the bodies of insects that were trapped in the sticky resin before it hardened. The ancient Greeks polished amber and used it for beads. It is often used to make jewelry today. More than 2,500 years ago, the Greeks discovered that when amber was rubbed with fur, it attracted small pieces of straw and made crackling sparks of static. The word "electricity" comes from the Greek word for amber, *elektron*.

ALSO READ: ELECTRICITY, FOSSIL.

AMBULANCE An ambulance, with its lights flashing and its siren wailing, may someday save your life. An ambulance is a "moving hospital." It is a car designed to give first aid to people who are injured in accidents, or who suddenly become very sick. Ambulances carry injured and sick people to hospitals.

The first ambulances were made to follow armies. Before then, wounded soldiers were either carried from the battlefield by their comrades or left lying where they fell until the fighting stopped. Napoleon's personal surgeon, Baron Dominique Jean Larrey, introduced the first ambulances to the French army in 1792. They were light carriages, each pulled by a single horse. They quickly took the wounded from the battlefield.

Ambulances drawn either by horses or mules carried wounded soldiers during the American Civil War. A plan for an ambulance corps was proposed in Congress in 1862. But Congress did not give its approval until 1865, when the war was ending. So the corps played little part in the war.

Many hospitals in the United States began to develop ambulance services after the Civil War. Cincinnati General Hospital was one of the first. Bellevue Hospital in New York also started an ambulance service. Michael Reese Hospital in Chicago was probably the first U.S. hospital to use motor-driven ambulances, in 1899. Since about 1950, helicopters have often been used as ambulances and have saved many lives.

Ambulances played an important part in both the World Wars of the present century. They were used on the battlefield, and also in cities to aid victims of bombing.

Large ambulances today are equipped to handle various kinds of medical emergencies. They carry bandages, drugs, oxygen masks, splints, *resuscitators* (breathing machines), and more. Ambulance attendants with medical training, called *paramedics*, are ready to give emergency treatment as the ambulance speeds to the hospital's emergency room. There are also airplanes specially converted to serve as air ambulances.

ALSO READ: HOSPITAL.

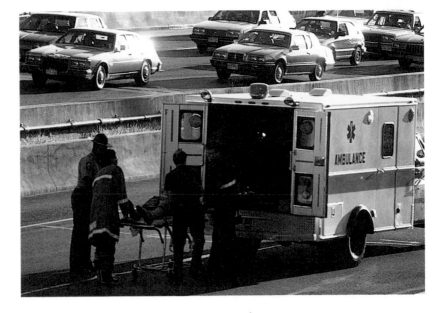

▲ *In an ambulance paramedics take care of the patient on the way to the hospital. This ambulance is attending an accident on an expressway.*

AMENDMENT see CONSTITUTION, UNITED STATES.

AMERICA The United States is often called "America," but this name really belongs to two great continents of the Western Hemisphere—North America and South America. Part of North America, the seven countries from Guatemala to Panama, is called Central America.

The two continents stretch 9,500 miles (15,288 km) from north to south. They vary in width from just 30 miles (48 km) in Panama to more than 4,000 miles (6,440 km) across Alaska and Canada. Millions of years ago, the two continents were separate. Then volcanoes spilled lava that formed the narrow, connecting link known as Central America.

The Americas were explored thousands of years ago by groups of Asian people. Some of them were the ancestors of the Indians and Eskimos of today. For centuries, Europeans did not know that the Americas existed. Vikings visited eastern Canada about A.D. 1000, but their settlements died out. In 1492, Columbus reached the Caribbean islands but thought he was in Asia. A later explorer, Magellan, sailed around the southern tip of the

Potatoes, tobacco, corn, tomatoes, lobsters, and other foods were brought back to Europe from America. In return, Europeans introduced pigs, cattle, horses, poultry, and cereal grains. These exchanges greatly shaped the habits of both Old and New Worlds.

Americas and across the Pacific. Europeans then realized that these lands were two new continents.

An Italian merchant named Amerigo Vespucci persuaded Spanish and Portuguese sea captains to take him along when they visited South America. He returned to Europe and wrote colorful letters claiming he had discovered a new world. One of these letters reached a German geography professor who named the Brazil area *America* (from Amerigo), in honor of Vespucci. The name became popular, and later became the name of both continents.

■ LEARN BY DOING

Imagine you could travel back in time. It would be exciting to discover a new world. Which of the first explorers of America would you choose to be? Maybe an Indian, journeying across the land bridge from Asia? How about Leif Ericson, or Columbus, or Amerigo Vespucci? You could write a history of your adventure. ■

ALSO READ: CENTRAL AMERICA; EXPLORATION; INDIANS, AMERICAN; NORTH AMERICA; SOUTH AMERICA; VIKINGS.

AMERICAN COLONIES The discovery and exploration of North America caused great excitement among seafaring people of Europe. They looked upon America as a New World, as a "land of opportunity." Most of all, they saw it as a source of marvelous treasures. Many of the leading European nations were eager to get the valuable furs, important minerals, and other useful natural resources of North America, so they could grow rich and powerful. They dreamed especially of discovering huge fortunes in gold, silver, and precious gems.

The Spanish were first in the rush to claim some of the riches of North America. They established the first permanent North American fort at St. Augustine, Florida, in 1565. English colonies were not started until after 1600. The French made a claim to Canada and most of the Mississippi Valley. The Dutch got hold of the lands along the Hudson River, and the Swedes took over the region of the Delaware River.

Britain was the most successful of all the nations competing for America's vast wealth. The colonists from France and Spain were interested mainly in trading with the Indians and taking gold and furs back to Europe. But the British colonists were determined to set up permanent homes in the New World. In time, Britain gained control of a large area of land along the Atlantic coast—including the regions that had first

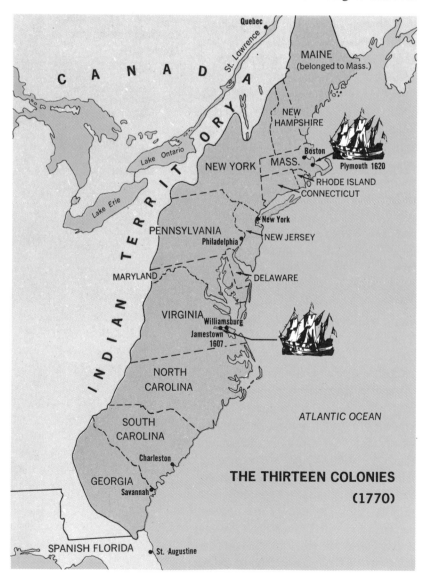

THE THIRTEEN COLONIES (1770)

been claimed by the Dutch and Swedes. Britain had established 13 permanent colonies by 1733. In the North were the *New England colonies*—Massachusetts, Connecticut, New Hampshire, and Rhode Island. The *middle colonies* were New York, Delaware, Pennsylvania, and New Jersey. The *southern colonies* were Virginia, Maryland, North Carolina, South Carolina, and Georgia. These colonies later became the 13 original United States of America.

The Early Settlements A large group of men and boys landed at Virginia in the spring of 1607. They founded the Jamestown Colony, the first permanent British settlement in the New World. A second group of people, the Pilgrims, sailed on the *Mayflower* from Plymouth, England, to the coast of Massachusetts in 1620. There they set up the Plymouth Colony. Puritans came from Britain ten years later to found the Massachusetts Bay Colony, with settlements in Boston and Salem.

Many hardships and dangers awaited these Europeans who first made the long ocean voyage to the New World. America of the 1600's was a vast wilderness. The colonists had to get used to this strange New World. They had to give up many of their Old World habits of living. Even the kinds of food they were used to eating were no longer available to them.

The Indians often lent a helping hand to the colonists. Indians had already explored most of the land, and they knew the best ways to travel the waters and cross the mountains. They showed the colonists where to find minerals and other important resources. They also knew all about the kinds of foods that could be found. The Massachusetts colonists had never even heard of such vegetables as corn, squash, and sweet potatoes. The Indians showed them how to grow these crops and to prepare foods

such as samp, corn pone, hominy, succotash, and popcorn.

But many Indian tribes were not so friendly to the newcomers. They were angry because the white men had forced them out of their homes and hunting grounds. They fought back with all their might. Men and boys in Virginia and Massachusetts had to learn to defend their homes and families from Indian attacks.

Not all the early settlers were prepared for the tough and dangerous life in Colonial America. The Jamestown colonists suffered from the burning heat of summer and the damp cold of winter. They worked hard. Many died of starvation and disease. But luckily, most of the early colonists were brave and hardy folk. They were ready to face all hardships in the struggle to build a new life in the land of opportunity. Many Europeans hoped to make new lives in the New World, so the settlement of America grew quickly after the founding of the earliest colonies. By 1700, the whole eastern coast was peppered with towns.

The People of the Colonies Most colonial settlers were English, but

▲ *Sir Walter Raleigh attempted to establish a colony in Virginia.*

▲ *In the 1500's, the Iroquois Indians of North America united together to protect themselves against the threat of invasion by white settlers.*

Colony	Date Founded	Founder	Reason for settlement	Statehood
Virginia	1607	Capt. John Smith	Profit and trade	June 25, 1788
Massachusetts	1620	William Bradford	Freedom to be Puritans	Feb. 6, 1788
New York	1626	Peter Minuit	Profit and trade	July 26, 1788
New Hampshire	1630	John Mason	Left Massachusetts because rules were too strict	June 21, 1788
Maryland	1634	George Calvert	Freedom to be Roman Catholics	Apr. 28, 1788
Connecticut	1636	Thomas Hooker	Left Massachusetts because rules were too strict	Jan. 9, 1788
Rhode Island	1636	Roger Williams	Thrown out of Massachusetts because he did not conform to Puritan thinking	May 29, 1790
Delaware	1638	Peter Minuit	Profit and trade	Dec. 7, 1787
North Carolina	1653	Eight Lords Proprietors	Profit and trade	Nov. 21, 1789
New Jersey	1664	John Berkeley and George Carteret	Profit and trade	Dec. 18, 1787
South Carolina	1670	Eight Lords Proprietors	Profit and trade	May 23, 1788
Pennsylvania	1682	William Penn	Freedom to be Quakers	Dec. 12, 1787
Georgia	1733	James Oglethorpe	Colonization	Jan. 2, 1788

▲ *This splendid doll was made in colonial times. It is dressed in a plaid cotton dress and straw hat.*

many others were French, Irish, Scottish, Dutch, German, and Swedish. They all had one thing in common—they wanted to make new lives for themselves. Some were drawn to the New World by the promise of work, because in their home countries they were not able to make a good living. Others were excited by the chance to get some land to call their own. The New World offered lands that were cheap, or even free. Still others fled Europe because they were not allowed to worship as they wished there. They hoped to find freedom of religion in the New World colonies. The Pilgrims and the Puritans had been the first religious groups to come to America for this reason. Others were the Quakers, Roman Catholics, and French Protestants known as Huguenots.

Some Europeans who wanted to settle in the New World were poor people who did not have enough money to make the trip. So they offered themselves as *indentured servants* to wealthy colonists. An indentured servant agreed to work for his master for a certain number of years. In return, the master agreed to pay

for the servant's trip and to provide him with room and board for the period of his service. But not all indentured servants came to America by choice. Some were criminals who had been forced to leave their countries. A few were black people brought from Africa by white Europeans. Many more blacks were captured in Africa and sold into slavery. Most of the slaves were brought to the southern colonies, to work on the farms. Other slaves were taken to the North and put to work in the homes or shops.

Everyday Life Each one of the three regions—New England, the middle colonies, and the southern colonies—had special conditions that made it different from the others. So people in each region developed different ways of living and working.

All the colonies depended on farming. The South was best suited for large-scale farming. The soil was rich and the climate was warm. Many southern colonists lived on huge plantations where tobacco and rice were grown for export to Britain. Every southern plantation was a tiny village.

The plantation owner, or planter, was mayor, judge, sheriff, preacher, doctor, lawyer, and storekeeper for the community. He and his family often lived in a great mansion. His black slaves lived in small shacks away from the main house. Most of them spent their days at hard labor in the fields. Some were put to work as servants in the planter's home.

Each plantation had its own carpenter, cooper (barrel-maker), blacksmith, cobbler (shoemaker), tanner, and other craftsmen who provided the basic needs of everyday life. From the plentiful plantation trees came the wood for the carpenter and the cooper. The blacksmith used wood for charcoal, which is needed to make ironware. Cotton and flax were grown and made into thread for weaving cloth. Cattle supplied milk and meat, as well as skins for the tanner and leather for the cobbler. Sheep's wool was woven or knitted to make clothing and bedding. Some planters were so rich they did not have to wear homemade clothing. They ordered fine silk gowns, satin breeches, and other fancy clothes from Britain.

The land in New England was rocky, the soil was poor, and the farms were small. Most towns were two rows of wooden or stone houses facing a *common* (a piece of land shared by the community) on which livestock grazed. Unlike the plantation family, the New England family did not raise crops for export to Britain. Each family grew only enough food for itself. The New Englander hardly ever bought ready-made British goods. People made all their own tools, clothing, and furniture. The North was blessed with rich forests, so there was plenty of lumber. New England woodworkers made especially fine furniture.

The main profit of the northern colonies came not from the land, but from the sea. Fishing, shipbuilding, shipping, and whaling were all important industries. Trading ships made

voyages along the Atlantic coast, bringing goods to the other colonies. They also crossed the Atlantic and traded with Europe, Africa, and the West Indies. Whaling ships sailed out of Nantucket, New Bedford, and other New England ports. Voyages sometimes lasted two or three years. One lasted eleven years!

The middle colonies were known as the 'bread" colonies. Their most important export was wheat. They also kept livestock and produced beef, pork, and lamb. Most of the farms were run by single families. But in the Hudson River Valley were large estates where wealthy landowners lived as comfortably as the planters of the South. The rich merchants of the cities also lived in splendid style.

Transportation The early colonists traveled by foot over the Indian paths and wilderness trails, or they rode horseback. For many years, there were no roads outside cities. People found it easier to travel by water than by land. Vessels sailed regularly up and down the coast from port to port. Inland, large rivers, such as the Hudson, were heavily traveled.

Overland travel became easier as city streets were paved with cobblestones and wilderness trails were made into dirt roads. In 1732, a stage-

▲ *The kitchen was the center of family life in most colonial homes. Every kitchen had a fireplace. With its crane and spit, the fireplace was used for cooking as well as heating. This is the kitchen at Wythe House in Colonial Williamsburg.*

▼ *Bacon's Castle, Virginia, was built in 1655. The Virginia Company was given a charter by King James I in 1606, and English colonists settled in Virginia a year later.*

In 1606 the east coast of North America was an almost unbroken wilderness. There were no Europeans except for a small group of Spaniards at St. Augustine, Florida. By 1750, less than 150 years later, there were over 1½ million men, women and children living in the 13 colonies.

▲ *American colonists had to do many jobs for themselves. Here, a man dressed in colonial clothes shows the art of flaxbreaking. The flaxbreak separates linen fiber from its woody core to prepare the fiber for spinning into thread.*

coach journeyed between New York and Philadelphia in record time—one week. Wealthy colonists imported splendid coaches from Europe. These coaches must have been a grand sight, painted with shiny gold and red paint, and drawn by four prancing horses.

But colonists who walked in the cities did not always have such a grand time. City streets were often used as garbage dumps. Hogs and other animals ran free in New York's streets, looking for food among the garbage. Rich people were able to buy *sedans* to avoid all this. The sedan was an enclosed chair with two poles attached to each side. Servants or slaves carried the chair, with its rider, on their shoulders.

School and Church Colonial children helped their parents with everyday chores. But schooling was also an important part of daily life for many children. The three R's—"Reading, 'Riting, and 'Rithmetic"—were the basic lessons taught by every school teacher, whether he or she was teaching in a public school or was hired as a private tutor. America's first public schools were in New England. The schools were free, but only boys could attend. Girls were rarely sent to public schools in colonial times. But both boys and girls could attend a "dame" school, run by a woman who taught in her home. The children learned their three R's seated around the kitchen fire. They made their own pens by carving sharp points from goose quills. They boiled bark to make a syrup that they used as ink.

On southern plantations, the planter's children were tutored by a schoolmaster who lived with the family for several months of the year. Some boys—and a few girls—were sent to private schools in Europe. The first free school in the South was the grammar school at the College of William and Mary, in Williamsburg, Virginia.

Going to church was another important part of colonial life. The church was not only a place of worship—it was also the center of community life. People in the South enjoyed staying around the church after the services were over. Adults gathered in groups to chat, while boys and girls played tag or hopscotch or flew kites. But the mood in New England churches on Sunday was quite different. The Puritans believed that people should be quiet and serious on the Sabbath. Children were not allowed to shout and play. Every Sunday morning, after the drum roll that announced the beginning of church services, every man, woman, and child had to be in his or her seat at the meeting house. Sermons often lasted three hours in the morning and another three hours in the afternoon.

Recreation Life in colonial times offered many pleasures as well as duties. Fox hunting, horse racing, and week-long house parties made life gay. New England parties were happy occasions that often combined work and play. Neighbors gathered together to husk corn, make quilts, and even build houses.

Like today's Americans, the early colonists especially enjoyed their holidays. Thanksgiving was first observed by the early settlers at Plymouth. But the colonists did not celebrate Christmas as this holiday is celebrated today. For the Puritans believed that it was wrong to be joyful about religion. Christmas did not become a real holiday until the middle of the 1800's. An important holiday in colonial times was the king's birthday.

In time, however, the links with the old homeland, Britain, became strained. The American colonists wanted more freedom to govern their own affairs. This desire grew stronger and stronger, until the colonists declared their break with British rule. A total of 169 years had passed between the time of the first permanent colony, at Jamestown in 1607, and the Declaration of Independence from Britain in 1776. After the 13 colonies won their right to be an independent nation, a happy day on the American calendar was Independence Day, the Fourth of July.

ALSO READ: AGRICULTURE; AMERICAN HISTORY; AMERICAN REVOLUTION; DECLARATION OF INDEPENDENCE; JAMESTOWN; MAYFLOWER; MAYFLOWER COMPACT; PILGRIM SETTLERS; PURITAN; RALEIGH, SIR WALTER; and the articles on each state shown on the table.

AMERICAN HISTORY Britain did not start to colonize the east coast of North America until more than a century after Columbus and other explorers had begun their explorations of the Western Hemisphere. The first permanent British settlement in the New World was started in 1607 at Jamestown in Virginia. The Virginia Colony was governed by the British governor and the House of Burgesses. The people elected the *burgesses* (representatives) to this assembly beginning in 1619. The Virginia House of Burgesses was the first representative assembly in America.

A second British settlement was started when the Pilgrims landed at Plymouth, Massachusetts, in 1620. The Pilgrims had left home because they were not allowed to worship God in their own way. They were part of a large group of people called *Puritans*, who wanted to "purify" the Church of England. Another group of Puritans founded the Massachusetts Bay Colony at Boston and Salem in 1630. The British had set up 13 colonies along the Atlantic Coast, from Maine to Georgia, by 1733.

Many North American Indians were friendly to the settlers and helped them learn the ways of the new land. But often bloody fights broke out between the colonists and the Indians. The Indians fought be-cause the colonists were taking over their lands.

The Roots of Revolution Wars fought by Spain, France, and Britain caused fighting in several parts of America during most of the 1700's. In America these were called the French and Indian Wars. Both the French and the British had Indians fighting for them. France lost the French and Indian Wars, and by 1763 Great Britain had gained nearly all French land in America, including Canada. The British needed money to pay their war debts. So Parliament decided to tax the colonies. The angry American colonists felt the taxes were unfair, because they had no representatives in Parliament. But even though they protested, King George III and Parliament would not end the taxes. Colonists who took the side of the king were called *Loyalists* or *Tories*. Other colonists wanted independence from Britain. They were called *Patriots*. Still others—probably a majority—had a "wait and see" attitude.

The Patriots felt that Britain was taking away rights that they deserved as free citizens. They could not get enough help from the British Parlia-

▲ *An Indian chief drawn in about 1585. As settlers moved westward and took over the most fertile land, they came into conflict with the Indians.*

▼ *A model of the "Santa Maria," the ship in which Christopher Columbus made his first Atlantic crossing in 1492.*

▲ *Two of the many different North American shelters: a bark tepee built by Cree Indians, and a Creek Indian house of branches.*

▲ *Early Puritan settlers in North America. They went there from England so that they could worship God in the way they wanted.*

▲ *Covered wagons, drawn by oxen or horses, carried pioneers westward. Settlers survived through their skills as hunters and farmers.*

ment, or from the king and his ministers. The colonists, therefore, defied the British government. This was particularly true in Massachusetts and in the city of Boston, beginning about 1761. Resistance had spread to other large cities by 1765. It continued to grow for ten years.

The Fight for Independence One night in April, 1775, the Patriots learned that British troops planned to capture guns and ammunition stored by the colonists in Concord, Massachusetts. Leaders of the Patriots were in danger of arrest, so Paul Revere and other Minutemen rode for miles through the darkness to warn them. The American Revolution began the next day at the Battles of Lexington and Concord.

The fighting lasted for almost seven years, during which George Washington was the commander in chief of the Continental Army. He kept the soldiers of the ill-equipped colonial army together until they won the war in 1781. In the peace treaty, signed in 1783, Great Britain recognized the independence of the United States of America, and turned over to the new country all British lands east of the Mississippi.

A national flag for the new United States was approved on June 14, 1777, during the Revolution. This first flag, the original Stars and Stripes, had one star for each state and 13 stripes to stand for the first 13 colonies.

The new nation needed laws to guide and protect its people. A first attempt at setting up a system of national law was made in the Articles of Confederation, which became law in 1781. But the system did not work, and a new Constitution of the United States was created in 1787. Adopted in 1789, it is still the basic law of the land today. Under the Constitution, a President is elected by the people every four years. The country called on George Washington again. He was

elected the first President and took office on April 30, 1789.

The Union Expands Not all Americans were content to live in the settled areas of the eastern coast. Looking for land to farm, some began to move west toward the Ohio River even before the Revolution. The land between the Appalachian Mountains and the Mississippi River was quickly settled. It was soon divided up into states, which joined the Union. By 1800, three more states—Vermont, Kentucky, and Tennessee—had joined the original 13.

The size of the country was more than doubled in 1803 by the Louisiana Purchase. The U.S., under the leadership of President Thomas Jefferson, paid France 15 million dollars for a huge tract of land that extended from the Mississippi River west to the Rocky Mountains, and from New Orleans all the way to Canada. Two young army officers, Meriwether Lewis and William Clark, explored this new land for the U.S. Government. Lewis and Clark traveled beyond the Rockies to the Pacific Ocean. Their glowing reports of the western frontier made many Americans decide to move west.

The United States and Britain went to war again in 1812, fighting over the freedom of U.S. ships at sea. U.S. troops burned government buildings at York (now Toronto) in Canada. In August, 1814, the British burned the U.S. Capitol, some other buildings, and the President's House in return. President James Madison had the house painted white to cover the scars and smoke stains. The home of the President of the United States has been called the "White House" since that time.

The U.S. continued to grow in size and political power after the War of 1812. Spain sold Florida to the U.S. in 1819. Settlements were founded beyond the Mississippi by pioneers who traveled to the West in wagon trains. Many Americans settled in Texas, which belonged to Mexico at that time. They fought with the Mexicans over laws and boundaries. In San Antonio, in 1836, an entire group of Texan Americans was killed by Mexican soldiers in the Battle of the Alamo. Angry Texans crying, 'Remember the Alamo!'' defeated the Mexicans a few weeks later. The Texans then went on to win their independence from Mexico. Texas was *annexed*, or added, to the Union as a state in 1845. The U.S. and Mexico fought over this annexation in the Mexican War from 1846 to 1848. The U.S. won. Mexico agreed to sell much of its western land, including California, to the U.S.

In 1849, gold was discovered in the new U.S. land of California. Many people, called 'Forty-Niners,'' went west in the search for gold. Other travelers to the West went to make new lives for themselves and their families. The trip westward was long and dangerous. The Oregon Trail, which many of these pioneers took,

was more than 2,000 miles (3,220 km) long. Indian attacks troubled almost every wagon train.

The Civil War In the first half of the 1800's, debate between the North and the South on the question of slavery became more and more bitter. Slaves brought from Africa had been used on the large plantations in the South since colonial times. When cotton became a popular crop, more and more slaves were needed. The South's prosperity was based on the slavery system. In the North, slavery was not profitable and most Northern states had laws against it. A large group of Northerners believed that slavery should not be allowed in new territories. They wanted to *abolish* (get rid of) slavery in the whole country. They were known as *abolitionists*. States' rights became a major issue. The Southern states saw less and less reason for staying in the Union.

In 1860—the year Abraham Lincoln was elected President—several southern states *seceded from* (left) the

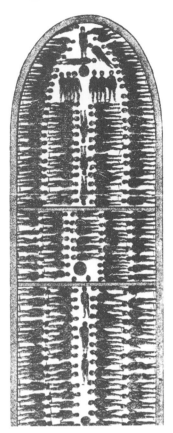

▲ *Slave ships packed like this sailed from Africa to the United States in the early 1800's.*

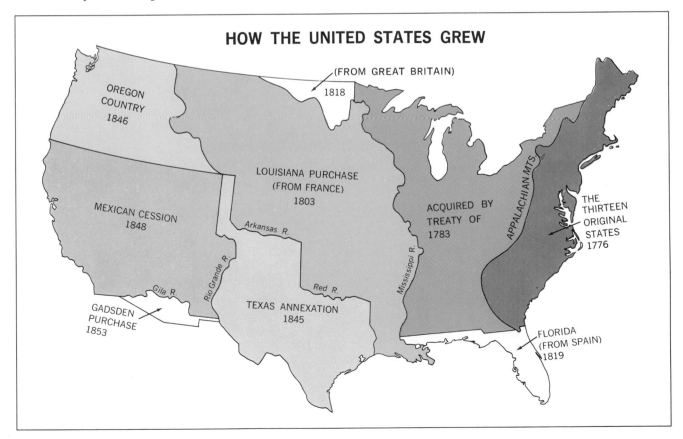

HOW THE UNITED STATES GREW

OREGON COUNTRY 1846

(FROM GREAT BRITAIN) 1818

MEXICAN CESSION 1848

LOUISIANA PURCHASE (FROM FRANCE) 1803

Arkansas R.

ACQUIRED BY TREATY OF 1783

APPALACHIAN MTS.

THE THIRTEEN ORIGINAL STATES 1776

Rio Grande R.

Gila R.

Red R.

Mississippi R.

GADSDEN PURCHASE 1853

TEXAS ANNEXATION 1845

FLORIDA (FROM SPAIN) 1819

▲ *A new nation's victory. The British surrender to the American forces at Yorktown.*

▶ *First President of the new republic, George Washington.*

▲ *A nation divided by war between North and South.*

▼ *The first telephone call on the new New York to Chicago line in 1892.*

▲ *America takes wing. And the Wright brothers write a new page in history.*

▼ *Henry Ford and other automakers sent a nation off on a new craze—the automobile.*

AMERICAN HISTORY TIMETABLE

Peopling a wilderness
Over 25,000 years ago the first people to settle North America travel across the land bridge linking the continent to Asia

1400's–1600's
First European exploration
First English settlement, at Jamestown, 1607
Pilgrims sail to Massachusetts, 1620
New York founded, 1624

1630–1760's
The colonies grow
From 1650 to 1750 the population of the colonies increases from 52,000 to 1,600,000.

1775–1789
A new nation is born
Declaration of Independence, 1776
Revolutionary War ends with British surrender at Yorktown, 1781

1803–1900
A century of expansion
Louisana Purchase, 1803, doubles the size of the country
War with Mexico 1846–48
California Gold Rush 1849
Alaska purchase, from Russia, 1867
First railroad link across the country, 1869
Civil War, 1861–65, followed by the years of Reconstruction
Many immigrants from Europe settle in the United States, 1840–1900

1870–1920
Industrial growth
Invention speeds the nation's progress:
Electric light, 1879; telephone, 1892; first airplane flight, 1903; Ford Model T, 1908. United States at war; World War I, 1917–18

1920–1945
Prosperity, depression, war
After 1920's Boom comes Depression of 1930. New Deal helps restore confidence
World War II, and United States at war following Pearl Harbor, 1941

1945–today
A world power
Atomic age, 1945
Korean War 1950–53
Supreme court rules against segregation, 1954
First U.S. space satellite, 1958
Vietnam War, 1968–73
Moonlanding, Apollo 11 1969

▲ *Uncle Sam called volunteers to fight in World War I.*

▼ *World War II saw the attack by the Japanese on Pearl Harbor.*

▲ *Lean years between world wars: the economic depression of the 1930's.*

▲ *The nation was divided over the rights and wrongs of the Vietnam War.*

▶ *President Kennedy vowed to send Americans to the moon, opening a new era in exploration.*

When the Civil War began, President Lincoln hoped that he would need only 75,000 volunteers for a few months to put down the uprising. In the end, four million men fought in a cruel war that lasted for four long years.

Union and formed a new government. They called themselves the Confederate States of America. They chose Jefferson Davis as their president. The Civil War began on April 12, 1861, when Confederate soldiers fired on a U.S. fort, Fort Sumter, in the harbor of Charleston, South Carolina.

Abraham Lincoln remained President of the U.S. throughout the four-year war. General Ulysses S. Grant was the most famous of the commanders of the Union forces. Robert E. Lee was the commanding general of the Confederate army. In this war, brother often fought against brother, and friend against friend. After the North won this long and bloody war, two things were settled—slavery was abolished, and it was clear that no state could leave the Union. Just five days after the Civil War ended, President Lincoln was assassinated in Ford's Theater in Washington, D.C. by John Wilkes Booth, an actor who was a strong supporter of the South.

The Railroad Helps Settle the West
The U.S. went through a period of prosperity for the next 20 years, mostly due to the growth of transportation. Railroads were built, running all the way to the Pacific coast. This

opened up the West for further settlement. Cattle raising, land development, lumbering, and silver mining made the western lands prosperous.

But the new settlers, miners, and ranchers posed a serious threat to the Indians. The American Indians were fighting not only for their lives, but for their way of life. They were being driven from their ancient hunting grounds, from the homelands that had been theirs for generations. One tribe that fought the hardest was the Apache. The Apache War raged in New Mexico, Arizona, and Texas. It lasted almost 40 years, and was probably the bloodiest Indian war. Other serious Indian wars were the Sioux War in North and South Dakota, Minnesota, and Montana; the Nez Percé War in the Pacific Northwest; and the Modoc War in California.

In the East, where manufacturing had become the most important business, another kind of fight was going on. The long struggle between factory owners and workers had started. Labor unions were seeking better working conditions, higher pay, and shorter hours for workers.

By 1890 there was scarcely any frontier (completely unsettled land) left. The nation stretched from the Atlantic to the Pacific. Forty-five states had been formed by the time the 20th century started. Three more states came into the Union in the next 12 years. The admission of huge Alaska and distant Hawaii in 1959 brought the number to 50 states.

A World Power Another war took place before the end of the 1800's. The Spanish-American War, fought with Spain in 1898 over Cuba's independence, began when a U.S. battleship, the *Maine*, was blown up in the harbor of Havana, Cuba. America won this brief conflict, and the world began to realize that the young country was becoming a power to reckon with. Under President Theodore Roosevelt, the U.S. dug the Panama

▼ *During the Depression years of the 1930's hunger and unemployment brought hardship to many Americans.*

Canal, which made it possible for ships to go from the Atlantic to the Pacific without going around stormy Cape Horn at the southern tip of South America.

World War I started in Europe in 1914. Germany fought against France and Britain. America did not want to enter this war at first. But events forced the country to fight. President Woodrow Wilson and Congress declared war on Germany in April, 1917. With fresh American troops helping out, Germany was defeated in 1918.

For more than ten years the world tried to recover from the debts and social changes brought about by the war. But finally there was a worldwide economic depression. The Depression began in the U.S. in 1929. Many people did not have jobs or money during this time, and they could not buy food or clothing. The government started many new building projects to make work so that people could earn at least some money. Highways, dams, bridges, and public buildings were constructed.

The U.S. was at peace with the rest of the world for 20 years after World War I. Then in 1939 World War II broke out in Europe. Germany, under Adolf Hitler and his Nazi party, aided by Italy, attacked and captured many European and North African countries. The U.S. still did not want to enter another world war. But the

Japanese, who were allies of the Germans and Italians, bombed the American naval base at Pearl Harbor, Hawaii, on December 7, 1941. Congress declared war on Japan, Germany, and Italy. Not until the Germans surrendered in May, 1945, was the war over in Europe. Japan did not surrender until August of that year, after the U.S. had dropped the first atom bombs on two Japanese cities.

One of the results of World War II was the organization of the United Nations. Nearly all the countries of the world belong to the UN. The representatives of the member nations work together to try to solve world problems. When war broke out between the North and South Koreans in 1950, the UN sent troops to defend the South Koreans from the North Korean Communists. The

The annual income of 240 million Americans is roughly equal to the total income of all the three billion people of Asia, Africa, and South America.

▼ *A U.S. soldier with a Vietnamese child. The Vietnam War was one of the great issues troubling the nation in the 1960's and early 1970's.*

U.S. gave the largest share of troops and equipment.

In spite of its war efforts, the United States had become more and more prosperous. Americans enjoyed a higher standard of living than any other people on Earth. Industry grew steadily through the 1950's.

Because of its position as the world's strongest and richest nation, the United States plays a leading part in world affairs. Its main rival in foreign affairs is the U.S.S.R. In the 1950's and 1960's U.S. personnel were sent to help the South Vietnamese in their war against the Communist North Vietnamese. By 1965 U.S. troops were fighting in Vietnam. The Vietnam War led to discontent at home. A peace accord was signed in 1973, to conclude the longest and unhappiest overseas war fought by Americans.

On July 20, 1969 two U.S. astronauts became the first men to walk on the moon. They left on the moon a sign which read, "We came in peace for all mankind." The U.S. has continued to advance in space technology, despite setbacks to its manned shuttle program. U.S. achievements in communications, computers, laser science, and microbiology in particular have been considerable. U.S. doctors have pioneered advanced surgery, such as organ transplants. Abroad, the U.S. has avoided further Vietnam-style involvements, but plays a major world role as one of the two super-powers.

For further information on:

Government, *see* ARTICLES OF CONFEDERATION; CABINET, U.S.; CONSTITUTION, U.S.; FLAG; UNITED STATES GOVERNMENT.

Life, *see* AMERICAN COLONIES; BLACK AMERICANS; EXPLORATION; HISPANIC AMERICANS; INDIANS, AMERICAN; PIONEER LIFE.

Major Events, *see* AMERICAN REVOLUTION, CIVIL RIGHTS MOVEMENT, CIVIL WAR, DEPRESSION, FRENCH AND INDIAN WAR, GOLD RUSH, INDIAN WARS, KOREAN CONFLICT, MEXICAN WAR, RECONSTRUCTION, SPANISH-AMERICAN WAR, WAR OF 1812, WORLD WAR I, WORLD WAR II, VIETNAM WAR.

Also read articles on each state and each President.

AMERICAN INDIAN   *see* INDIANS, AMERICAN.

AMERICAN REVOLUTION

"These United Colonies are, and of right ought to be Free and Independent States." So said the Second Continental Congress in the Declaration of Independence in 1776. Many events happened before the colonists were ready to take this stand. It took

Most people know the story of how Israel Putnam dropped his plow in the field and rode a day on horseback to Boston after hearing the news of the battle of Lexington. What is not so well known is that Putnam did volunteer and fight at Bunker Hill and elsewhere as a general in the American Revolution.

▶ *"Give me liberty or give me death." Patrick Henry uttered these famous words before a convention of Virginians in 1775. They expressed the mood of an America ready to fight for freedom.*

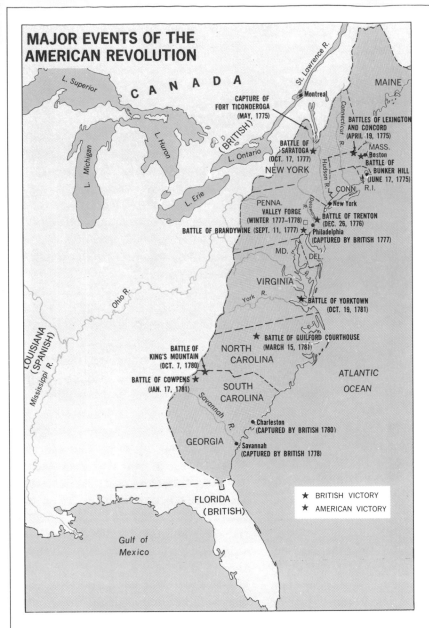

MAJOR EVENTS OF THE AMERICAN REVOLUTION

CANADA

L. Superior

L. Michigan

L. Huron

L. Ontario

L. Erie

Montreal

St. Lawrence R.

(BRITISH)

MAINE

CAPTURE OF
FORT TICONDEROGA
(MAY, 1775)

BATTLES OF LEXINGTON
AND CONCORD
(APRIL 19, 1775)

BATTLE OF
SARATOGA
(OCT. 17, 1777)

NEW YORK

MASS.
Boston

BATTLE OF
BUNKER HILL
(JUNE 17, 1775)

Hudson R.

Connecticut R.

CONN.

R.I.

New York

PENNA.
VALLEY FORGE
(WINTER 1777-1778)

BATTLE OF TRENTON
(DEC. 26, 1776)

BATTLE OF BRANDYWINE (SEPT. 11, 1777)

Delaware R.

Philadelphia
(CAPTURED BY BRITISH 1777)

MD.

DEL.

VIRGINIA

York R.

BATTLE OF YORKTOWN
(OCT. 19, 1781)

Ohio R.

BATTLE OF GUILFORD COURTHOUSE
(MARCH 15, 1781)

LOUISIANA
(SPANISH)

Mississippi R.

BATTLE OF
KING'S MOUNTAIN
(OCT. 7, 1780)

NORTH
CAROLINA

ATLANTIC
OCEAN

BATTLE OF COWPENS
(JAN. 17, 1781)

SOUTH
CAROLINA

Savannah R.

Charleston
(CAPTURED BY BRITISH 1780)

GEORGIA

Savannah
(CAPTURED BY BRITISH 1778)

★ BRITISH VICTORY

★ AMERICAN VICTORY

FLORIDA
(BRITISH)

Gulf of
Mexico

▲ *A group of patriotic Americans at the First Continental Congress in 1774. They came from far and wide to plan joint action against the British.*

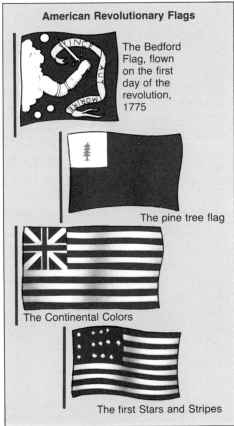

American Revolutionary Flags

The Bedford Flag, flown on the first day of the revolution, 1775

The pine tree flag

The Continental Colors

The first Stars and Stripes

◀ *The signing of the Declaration of Independence on July 4, 1776, was the highlight of the Revolution and the birth of a new nation. To all the world, it served notice of a new order—the rights of the people had now replaced the rights of kings.*

▶ *The Battle of Lexington, 1775. British troops fire their muskets at the fleeing Lexington militia.*

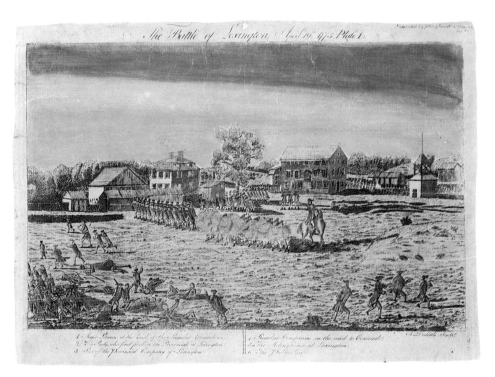

The Battle of Lexington, April 19, 1775. Plate 1.

The chief weapon used in the American Revolution was the flintlock musket with a bayonet. Each soldier carried cartridges of paper, lead balls, and black powder in a box slung over his shoulder.

When the original 13 colonies declared their independence in 1776, the United States was only a fourth of its present size. By 1850 it was a nation of 31 states stretching from the Atlantic to the Pacific, an area of 3 million square miles (nearly 8 million sq. km).

a long and hard struggle to make these words come true.

The British won the French and Indian War in 1763. They needed money to pay for the war and govern Canada and the eastern Mississippi Valley, which they had taken from the French. Parliament decided to raise funds by increasing taxes in the American colonies. The Stamp Act of 1765 required that tax stamps had to be bought for wills, deeds, and other legal documents. Every newspaper, magazine, almanac, or calendar sold in the colonies also had to be stamped. Americans were not allowed to have anyone represent them (speak and vote for them) when tax laws were made in Parliament. "No taxation without representation," was the cry of the angry colonists. They wanted the right to make their own laws, not to be ruled by the Parliament in Britain.

Trouble in Boston Another act of Parliament that the colonists hated was the Quartering Act. The colonies had to provide housing and supplies for British soldiers in America. The people of Boston and New York,

where many troops were stationed, were especially upset by this law. A noisy crowd of men and boys gathered near Boston's Customs House on a cold March day in 1770. Some of the boys threw snowballs at a British sentry. The sentry called for other soldiers, and the crowd became angrier and angrier. Shots rang out. Three Americans lay dead and eight were wounded (two of the wounded died later). Crispus Attucks, a leader of the crowd and probably a runaway slave, was the first to die. This incident was called the *Boston Massacre*.

The Boston colonists were spurred to violence again three years later, in December of 1773. The British shipped tea to America. The tea tax was small, but the colonists were not allowed to vote on the tax. The protest known as the Boston Tea Party was held when the ships arrived in Boston Harbor with their cargo. Colonists disguised as Indians dumped 342 chests of tea into the harbor. The British promptly closed Boston Harbor. The British governor sailed home, leaving General Thomas Gage in command. The Quartering Act, which had been stopped, was started again. And if a British official were charged with a crime against a colonist, he was not tried locally, but was sent to Britain for trial.

The people of Boston and of Massachusetts were angry. So were many other colonists. The First Continental Congress met in Philadelphia in September, 1774. Every colony except Georgia was represented. The Congress formed the Continental Association, adopted a declaration of rights, and decided not to import British goods. The delegates agreed to meet again the following May if Parliament did not rewrite the unjust laws.

The Shot Heard 'Round the World
In April, 1775, General Gage marched his British troops from Boston, through Lexington, to Concord. Spies had told the British commander that guns and ammunition were stored in Concord. These spies also told Gage that two patriot leaders, Samuel Adams and John Hancock, were hiding in Lexington. Gage planned to capture the supplies and the rebels. But the Americans also had spies. When the red-coated British started their secret march, two Americans saddled their horses and sped through the darkness to warn the colonists at Lexington and Concord that the British were coming.

Those heroic riders were Paul Revere and William Dawes. They were aided by Dr. Samuel Prescott, who took the warning to Concord after Revere was captured.

Gage's 700 or 800 redcoats met a band of Minutemen (farmers and shopkeepers who were ready at a minute's notice) lined up on Lexington's village green. No one knows who fired the first shot. But, in the shooting that followed, eight Americans were killed and the rest scattered. The British marched on to Concord. British troops did not find Adams, Hancock, or the supplies, because Dr. Prescott had warned the colonists in Concord.

The British dumped several barrels of flour and set fire to some buildings at Concord before starting back to Boston. The redcoats found their return route blocked by angry Minutemen. Aroused by the news of the Americans killed at Lexington, hundreds of farmers and merchants swarmed toward Concord. The British fought off an attack on Concord's North Bridge. But their return march became a nightmarish retreat. Rifles and muskets were fired from behind every stone wall, building, or brushpile that could hide a Minuteman. By the time the redcoats finally reached the safety of their barracks, 273 of

The Revolutionary War was a small war compared with modern ones. Large numbers of men were never involved. There were never more than 20,000 men in the American army. Estimates of the number of American soldiers killed in the war vary between 5,000 and 12,000.

◀ *The Battle of Bunker Hill was one of the first battles of the war. During this fight, when ammunition was scarce, the American colonel, William Prescott, told his men, "Don't shoot until you see the whites of their eyes."*

▲ *In this famous painting by Emanuel Leutze, George Washington is shown crossing the Delaware River on Christmas night, 1776, to attack Hessian soldiers in New Jersey.*

▶ *American commander John Paul Jones lashed his flagship* Bon Homme Richard *to the British warship* Serapis *and forced its surrender after three hours of bloody fighting.*

their number had been killed or wounded.

One month later, Ethan Allen and Benedict Arnold led the Green Mountain Boys in the capture of Fort Ticonderoga, the most important British fortress north of the Hudson River. News of their daring attack encouraged the delegates to the Second Continental Congress in Philadelphia. The Congress now had to deal with a real war, so they called for a real army. The Congress chose a wealthy planter from Virginia to command this Continental Army. He was well suited for the job. He had been a lieutenant colonel in Britain's wars with France, and he later led several companies of Virginia volunteer soldiers. His name was George Washington.

The first major battle of the war—the Battle of Bunker Hill—was fought on June 17, 1775. It actually took place on nearby Breed's Hill. The British captured the hill, but more than twice as many British soldiers were killed or wounded as Americans. Many American colonists—called Loyalists—were still against breaking away from Britain, even though battles had been fought and men killed. This deep-seated struggle between American Patriots and Loyalists went on throughout the Revolution.

The Declaration Leads to Full-Scale War The Continental Congress continued to hope until the summer of 1776 that Great Britain would be fair to the colonies. Then a delegate from Virginia finally offered a resolution for full independence. Thomas Jefferson wrote the first draft of the document that declared the colonies were free. John Adams and Benjamin Franklin made small changes. Other minor changes were made by the Congress. The Declaration of Independence was adopted in Philadelphia, on July 4, 1776.

That summer, the British shifted the fighting from Boston to New

York. Washington's army was pushed from Long Island and Manhattan by troops led by Sir William Howe. Washington was forced to retreat into New Jersey and then into Pennsylvania. Washington and his men crossed the ice-packed Delaware River on Christmas night, 1776, in open boats and captured the garrison at Trenton, New Jersey. The troops at Trenton were German soldiers, called Hessians, whom the British paid to fight for them. The Americans won a small victory a few days later at Princeton, New Jersey. The British then began a major attempt to capture Philadelphia, the colonial capital. Philadelphia was taken from American hands in the fall of 1777. This was a staggering blow. The Continental Congress moved the capital to York, Pennsylvania, about 80 miles (129 km) west of Philadelphia.

The Tide Turns The British tried to cut the colonies in half by advancing south from Canada with another army commanded by General John Burgoyne. But they were forced to surrender at the Battle of Saratoga in New York. This American victory was the turning point of the war. The

French became allies of the Americans after Saratoga. French soldiers, ships, and money aided the American cause. Spain also helped, and the Netherlands loaned money for the fight.

But the American cause was in danger during the dreadful winter of 1777–1778. The British held Philadelphia. The government was in exile at York. And General Washington was camped in the snow at Valley Forge. His men were starving and frozen. The young French nobleman, the Marquis de Lafayette, was barely 20 when he joined General Washington and spent that winter at Valley Forge. Lafayette did not believe that men could survive such misery and hardship. Washington stated in one report that 3,000 men could not fight because they had no shoes or warm clothing.

Baron von Steuben, a friend of Benjamin Franklin, brought hope and encouragement to the Americans in the spring of 1778. Von Steuben, a former Prussian (German) officer, trained the Continental soldiers until they became better fighters, both in groups and as individuals.

The American Navy had had only

▲ *A group of war-weary Americans encamped at Valley Forge. Although supplies were short, many men braved the terrible winter of 1777-78. They stayed with George Washington to fight again.*

It has been estimated that the Revolutionary War cost the United States about a hundred million dollars.

127

When the United States bought the Louisiana territory from France in 1803, it doubled its size overnight and added an area which made up almost 13 present-day states. The purchase cost about three cents an acre for what proved to be some of the richest food-producing land in the world.

four ships when the Revolution began. Congress later had more built. Many small, privately owned ships were used as *privateers*, seizing British supply and merchant ships. They also transported arms from France. John Paul Jones was a hero of the war at sea. With his ship, the *Bon Homme Richard*, he captured the British warship *Serapis* in a spectacular battle in 1779.

George Rogers Clark of Virginia captured several British forts in the region of Illinois and Michigan in 1778 and 1779. Clark's victories over the British and their Indian allies helped the Americans gain more favorable terms when the peace treaty was signed. Britain was forced to give all lands east of the Mississippi River to the Americans.

The British turned their efforts to the southern colonies in 1780 and 1781. They captured Savannah, Georgia, and won at Charleston, South Carolina. But they lost at Kings Mountain and Cowpens. American heroes of the South included Francis Marion, the 'Swamp Fox," whose guerrilla-like (hit-and-run) warfare confused the British troops, and led to their defeat.

Surrender at Yorktown Lord Cornwallis marched his British troops north and occupied Yorktown, in

midsummer of 1781. He wanted to help the Royal Navy control Virginia, Maryland, and the Chesapeake Bay.

General Washington and the French leader, Count Rochambeau, cornered the British troops with the help of Lafayette and "Mad Anthony" Wayne. The French navy, led by Admiral de Grasse, blocked escape by sea. Lord Cornwallis surrendered at Yorktown on October 17, 1781.

John Adams, Benjamin Franklin, and John Jay started peace talks for the Americans in April, 1782. When the Treaty of Paris was signed in September, 1783, Great Britain granted independence to the Americans and recognized the new United States of America.

For further information on:
Background, *see* AMERICAN COLONIES, BOSTON MASSACRE, BOSTON TEA PARTY, CONTINENTAL CONGRESS, DECLARATION OF INDEPENDENCE, FRENCH AND INDIAN WAR.
Leaders for Independence, *see* ADAMS, SAMUEL; FRANKLIN, BENJAMIN; HANCOCK, JOHN; HENRY, PATRICK; JEFFERSON, THOMAS; PAINE, THOMAS; REVERE, PAUL.
Leaders in War *see* ALLEN, ETHAN; CLARK, GEORGE ROGERS; HALE, NATHAN; JONES, JOHN PAUL; LAFAYETTE, MARQUIS DE; MARION, FRANCIS; WASHINGTON, GEORGE.

▶ *Supported by the French, Washington's American army compelled the British forces of Cornwallis to surrender at Yorktown, Virginia in October, 1781. The peace treaty was signed in 1783.*